God Answers
Moms
Prayers

How True,

Allison Bottke

with **Cheryll Hutchings**

D1056135

HARVEST HOUSE PUBLISHERS

EUGENE, OREGON

To protect the privacy of the individuals involved in the following stories, the names have been changed when deemed appropriate.

Cover by Left Coast Design, Portland, Oregon

GOD ANSWERS MOMS' PRAYERS
Copyright © 2005 by Allison Bottke
Published by Harvest House Publishers
Eugene, Oregon 97402
www.harvesthousepublishers.com

Library of Congress Cataloging-in-Publication Data
Bottke, Allison.
  God answers moms' prayers / Allison Bottke with Cheryll Hutchings.
     p. cm. — (God answers prayers)
  ISBN 0-7369-1588-5 (pbk.)
  1. Mothers—Religious life—Anecdotes. 2. Prayer—Anecdotes. I. Hutchings, Cheryll.
II. Title.
  BV4529.18B67 2005
  242'.6431—dc22

                                                                                    2004027209

Printed in the United States of America

05   06   07   08   09   10   11   12   / VP-CF /   10   9   8   7   6   5   4   3   2   1

In memory of Dolores Bandy Gappa—
We miss you, Mom.
Thank you for praying for us.

Contents

Foreword

I believe in the power of prayer. I have seen it with my own eyes. I have been in Moms In Touch prayer groups and in church mothering circles praying with other believing moms. When God answers prayers, I call them Mom's Mini Miracles. Maybe I have not seen the Red Sea part, but I have seen God open up doors of salvation, help, and opportunity.

For example, my most frantic mommy prayer was for my ADD/ADHD son. Zach and his hyperactivity continually kept me on my knees, but when he hit eight years old, I got seriously worried about his depressive behavior. He was spiraling down quickly. His grades were in the pits, his attitude in the dumps. He was angry, hostile, uncooperative, and a daily drain on the family. He was not a very verbal kid, so when he was upset, he would just start hitting whoever was around!

One day I walked into the living room, and Zach was giving his little brother a pounding for no reason at all.

"Zach, you need to go upstairs. This is inappropriate behavior. I will be right up to talk to you."

He stomped up the stairs, batting all the family photos off the wall as he went. He slammed the door to his room, picked up a baseball, and threw it *through* the door. I ran up the stairs after him.

"Zach! This is inappropriate! If you are upset, you have got to learn to use words!" (I was thinking, *At this rate, no woman will ever want to marry him, and he will live with me for the rest of his life!*)

"You want words! You want words!" he screamed back at me, his hands defiantly on his hips. "If you want words, then I hate myself! I hate my life! And if God made me, I hate Him, too! How's that for words?"

Shocked and stunned, I stood silent. Then I whispered, "Just a minute!"

I ran downstairs and threw myself to the floor, not on my knees in prayer, but flat on my face, begging God. "Lord, I am a pastor's wife, a director of women's ministries, and I write all these Christian books, but I am raising this wild little man of an atheist upstairs! I need some help here! I know Zach has a treasure inside him. Everyone has a uniqueness and calling on his or her life. But I can't see Zach's treasure, and Zach can't see his treasure, so help me help Zach see his treasure!"

When I said the word *treasure,* the Holy Spirit dropped an idea in my head: "Make a treasure map!" So I did! I drew up a map and took it upstairs.

"Zach, you have a unique treasure inside you. God places uniqueness in every person He creates, so you and I and God are going to go on a great adventure to discover that treasure.

"Every day I am going to ask you one thing you did well and one thing positive about your day, and we're going to record the answers on the treasure map. At the end of eight weeks we're going to see what patterns God is showing like a road map to your treasure. At the end of our journey, Mom will invest some money into buying you some resources to live out that treasured calling. Every week we'll go on a Mom-and-Son date, we'll pray, and God will show us your treasure."

Fast-forward ten years. We are in Dallas riding the elevator down to watch Zach perform at the National Co-Ed Cheerleading finals.

There was a hyper little boy in the elevator riding with his exhausted mom, who was leaning against the wall. He was jumping around hitting everyone in the elevator, until finally his exasperated mom barked out, "Zach!"

I said, "Zach! I have a Zach, too! He was once a hyper little guy like you, but right now we're going to see him perform. He's going to be on ESPN. He went from failing in school to discovering God made him special. He's the president of Fellowship of Christian Athletes, and he's just been offered a scholarship to cheer on the nation's number-one cheer team in college."

The mom stood up and said, "There *are* still miracles!"

Yes! There are still miracles, and on the pages of this book, *God Answers Moms' Prayers,* you will read about many mothers and be inspired by their stories. These are stories of mothers who dared to pray. You will read stories of women from all walks of life: birth moms, adoptive moms, spiritual and mentoring moms, all tied together with the miracle of answered prayer. Allison has done an amazing job gathering snapshots of answered prayers that *every* woman can relate to. You will want to share these stories with your favorite moms.

You will catch Allison's heartbeat on the pages because, after 35 years as a nonbeliever, Allison made an amazing U-turn toward God and has a passion to share God's grace, mercy, and love with other people. The stories in this book are not just feel-good, warm and fuzzy stories (there are plenty of those books around). The stories in *God Answers Moms' Prayers* have been selected for their ability to help you build a stronger faith. You will find yourself saying, "God helped them in this situation, and He can help me, too!" These are inspiring, life-changing, faith-building stories *by* moms and *about* moms and *for* moms. They are stories from God's heart to encourage your heart.

I know it is Allison's prayer that you will come to a better understanding of just how awesome is God's love for you and for those you love, and how He can and does provide for us.

That is my prayer for you as well. May God meet you on these pages and in your prayers.

—PAM FARREL, author of *The Treasure Inside Your Child; The 10 Best Decisions a Woman Can Make;* and *Men Are Like Waffles, Women Are Like Spaghetti*

Acknowledgments

Special blessings to our editorial team: Susan Fahncke, Cheryll Hutchings, Terri McPherson, and Sharen Watson.

God has often answered my prayers by bringing special people into my life—people who love and support me, pray with and for me, make me laugh and cry, and hold me accountable. While there is no way I could possibly thank everyone who made this book possible, I would like to extend warm, appreciative hugs to the following folks:

All of our contributing authors, God bless you! And thanks to Marlene Bagnull, the Bird family, Penny Carlevato, Jennifer Cary, Victor and Dorothy Constien, Lisa Copen, Mickey Crippen, Eva Marie Everson, Pam Farrel, Greg and Cathie Gappa, Heather Gemmen, Michelle McKinney Hammond, Nick Harrison, Cory Howard, Anne Johnson, LaRose Karr, Gene and Carol Kent, Ken Knight, Linda Lagnada, Jocelyn Lansing, Steve Laube, Florence Littauer, Marita Littauer, Don and Gladys Longpre, Lowell and Connie Lundstrom, Chip MacGregor, Carolyn McCourtney, Carolyn McCready, Mary McNeal, Dale Meyer, Diane O'Brian, Stormie Omartian, Susan Titus Osborn, Tracie Peterson, Marilyn Phillips, Linda Evans Shepherd, Betty Southard, Tammy Thorpe, Brad and Mary Utpadel, Thelma Wells, Sandra Wenker, Pamela Wetzell, Terry Whalin, and my AWSA Sisters, my CLASS family, the Masterpiece Studios crew, my Writers View sisters and brothers, and last but no means least, the very special God Allows U-Turns prayer team.

And to my children: Christopher Smith, Mandy Bottke, Kermit and Jennifer Bottke, and Kyle Bottke. My prayer is for your prayers to be answered. I love you.

Introduction

THERE IS A REASON BEHIND MY PASSION to share the life-changing, true stories of other people through the God Allows U-Turns books and the God Answers Prayers series. That reason is simply that *the power of God's truth changes lives*. And the power of prayer in affecting change is immeasurable, especially the prayers of a mother.

Many readers know my personal story about how I came to know the Lord at the age of 35. That story is the foundation of the entire God Allows U-Turns outreach. For those readers who are not familiar with my turbulent past, let me sum it up for you.

My parents divorced when I was young, leaving emptiness in my heart that I could never understand. As a teenager, I felt apart from girls my own age, and I rebelled strongly against any and all authority. I had given up on God long before I ran away at the age of 15 to marry the 18-year-old man who in one year went from being the love of my life to my abuser, jailer, kidnapper, rapist, and attempted murderer. By the time I was "Sweet 16," there was no doubt in my mind: If God existed, it was certainly not in my world.

After the birth of my son and my divorce, both at the age of 16, there was no room in my life for anything but the here and now. Practical things consumed me, like going back to school, working, childcare, housekeeping, and paying bills. I was so very lost.

I filled my days with busy, take-charge tasks. I filled my nights with alcohol, drugs, parties, and self-destruction. I filled my soul with empty promises and emptier pursuits. Over the years, another marriage and divorce, several broken engagements, more than one abortion, and frequent extreme weight gains and losses left me even more emotionally crippled.

Why couldn't I find happiness? Why did it seem as though nothing I did worked out? Why did I feel so worthless? The feelings of utter helplessness and hopelessness, of unrealized dreams, broken promises, and dead-end streets overwhelmed me.

Then one summer evening when I was taking a walk in my neighborhood, I noticed people going into the neighborhood church. Suddenly my legs developed a mind of their own, virtually propelling me up the steps and through the doors.

Alone in the church balcony, I looked toward the pulpit and saw the statue of Jesus with outstretched hands, looking right at me. Hot tears fell down my cheeks as emotions I could not explain filled my heart and soul.

What was wrong? What was happening to me? Why was I sitting in a strange church and crying like a baby? When the pastor began to speak, it was a message about being lost, without direction, without hope, without faith, and how it did not have to be like that. He talked of how we needed only to listen to the Holy Spirit and ask the Lord Jesus Christ to come into our hearts, and He would be there—just like that.

My walk with the Lord started that day—a day that forever changed the course of my life. Suddenly I wanted to know more about this relationship with Jesus of which the pastor spoke.

There it is, in the proverbial nutshell. Since that time, well over a decade ago, God has used my pathetic past to help change lives. He has given me a boldness to bare my soul in ways I could never have imagined. I could also never have imagined how God would answer my most fervent prayer: the prayer of my own heart for my lost son.

As a teenage mom I had been driven to show the world I could do it all. Escaping the battleground of abuse, I was convinced that love and hard work would see us through. "You and me against the world" was my mantra as I returned to school, entered the workforce, balanced an active social life, and discovered how temporarily comforting drugs, alcohol, and relationships could be when life got to be too much to handle on my own.

I ran my home like a military base: schedules, to-do lists, strict chores, and unreasonable expectations. My little boy never had a chance to be a little boy. My life was hard, and I needed him to grow up fast.

I thought I was doing a stellar job as a single mom. Mannerly, bright, precocious, and always clean, well-dressed, and well-fed, my son was a good boy, a handsome boy, a healthy boy. We did a lot of things together as he was growing up: museums, concerts, trips, lots of fun events. Learning was important to me, and I tried my best to instill a love of learning and adventure in my son. Yet day-care providers and my own mom helped to raise my son much of the time. That's because we lived a double life. At least I did. When I wasn't being super-mom, I was being "super party girl."

During the formative years of my son's life, I was desperate to fill the emptiness in my heart. When I wasn't filling that space with work or being a controlling mother, I filled it with drugs, alcohol, parties, relationships, and New Age spirituality. Psychic readings and tarot cards dictated how I lived. I justified my lifestyle because I did not "party" in front of my child. He was either asleep or with a sitter. I had worked hard to get off welfare, and I was not a deadbeat mom. I felt I deserved to have a good time. I wasn't hurting anyone, or so I thought.

I changed jobs and we switched apartments at the drop of a hat. I uprooted my son a dozen times before his twelfth birthday, never understanding the damage my lifestyle was doing to him.

Most damaging was my teaching that there was no God other than that which we manifested from within. "There is no God," I declared loudly and often.

When my son ran away from home the first time at the age of 13, I was bereft. While I was busy filling the emptiness in my heart, he had discovered a culture that brought comfort to him. The anarchistic punk movement in Huntington Beach, California, embraced him, and he was hooked. He had also become hooked on drugs—no doubt stealing pot from me, his own mother.

When the Lord finally got my attention, when I cried out to Him for help, my son had been arrested the day before for another juvenile infraction. He had been living on the streets on and off for five years. He was almost 18 years old. I was 34.

My first prayers as a new Christian were for my lost son. I begged God to forgive me for being such a pathetic excuse for a mother, for all the mistakes I had made, for raising an atheist whose only source of comfort had become the high he experienced from drugs and alcohol.

While I had been able to "control" my addictions, maintaining an apartment, a job, and the façade that I had it all together, my son could not. I lost my son for the next decade to heroin. Crime, cons, and corruption ruled his life. He was in and out of jail and homeless shelters, and living most of the time on the streets. Months would go by when I did not know where he was, or if he was even alive. It seemed to me that the stronger my walk with God became, the more Satan gripped my son's life.

All I could do was pray: on my knees, on my face, in my car, at work, and whenever thoughts of him entered my mind—which was often. Intercessors began to pray on my son's behalf: friends, church members, and writing groups. As the God Allows U-Turns book series began to grow, fellow readers and contributing authors banded together to pray for him as well.

Through it all my son continued to deny that God existed. "That's cool, Mom, that you found God, but it's not my thing," he would tell me whenever I broached the subject.

"Why do not you hear my prayers, God?" I would often cry. "Please do not take my son from me. Please give him—and me— another chance. Please save him!"

I bought a life-insurance policy for my son so I could afford to bury him when the time came, feeling certain that either drugs or crime would one day take his life. I prayed fervently for his safety on the streets and in jail. The first time I had to talk to him on a phone through a plate-glass window at a federal prison was more than I could bear. Seeing him in leg irons and handcuffs broke my heart. I wept so hard in the parking lot that I couldn't drive for over an hour. I felt in my heart if he did not make a U-turn soon, I would lose him forever.

What a mess I had made of his life! And it was then that God clearly talked to me.

"Remember what you tell people, Allison? Remember the cornerstone message of the U-Turns ministry?"

The choices you make change the story of your life, I thought in my mind.

"Christopher is a man now, Allison," the Lord impressed on my heart. "He's making his own choices now. Stop blaming yourself. Just give him to Me."

It was then that my prayers changed from, "Please, Lord, would You do this?" to "Thy will be done."

My own mother had prayed for me before my U-turn. Since then, we had prayed together for my son. The day she died, my son was in jail, awaiting sentencing that could mean 25 years behind bars. He was in another state, and I couldn't tell him in person about his beloved Gram. He had been so close to her during the years when I had been selfishly involved in my own messed-up life. I was trying to figure out how to tell him when his letter arrived.

The return address was a jail in Colorado. It was spring 2003, a few weeks after my mom had died.

The sun was warm. I had been working in the yard and sat down on the picnic-table bench to read. As I unfolded the letter, a small card fell to the ground. Reaching to pick it up, I saw my son's unmistakable signature on the line that read, "Today I make my profession of faith." It was dated April 7, 2003—the day we buried his beloved Gram.

My son had accepted Jesus. I had handed over my son to God, and my son had at last handed over his life to God.

I wept openly as I sat in my backyard, wishing my mom could be here to rejoice with me, yet knowing she was in heaven singing with the angels over this momentous occasion.

And for the first time in his life, my son began to pray.

"Mom, I am preparing myself for the worst. If I have to do 25 years behind bars, it's my own fault. God must have a plan for me to be here." What bittersweet words for a mom's ears.

That's when the miracles began to happen. My son was suddenly transferred to a small jail in Colorado, where each of the six inmates were Christians, and Bible study took up the majority of their day. "I've looked at Bibles in the past," he said to me on the phone one day, "and they never made sense. But now I get it!"

Within a few short weeks, the judge sentenced him to long-term residential treatment. A place opened up for him in an affordable program, and for the first time in his adult life, my son was free: free from the bondage of looking over his shoulder, free from drugs, free from Satan's hold on his life.

Washed in Jesus' blood, in my tears, and later in water as he was baptized at his request, my son entered his thirty-first year of life as a new man, in more ways than one. Today he lives nearby, has his own apartment, is gainfully employed, and knows God is with him.

God Answers Moms' Prayers holds a special place in my heart. I gave my son physical life, but God gave him so much more. As a young Christian, he still struggles with the ways of the world, just as I did when my U-turn was new. But I rest in the assurance that God has a powerful plan for this young man's life. I cannot control his walk of faith any more than I could control the path he eventually took toward self-destruction. I can worry about him, I can still shed tears over choices I am afraid will once again lead him astray, but God calls to me in that still, small voice saying, "Lean not on your own understanding, Allison, but in all ways acknowledge Me."

God has answered the prayer of my heart. He can do the same for you. I share this story with you for no other reason than to bring clarity to something that took me a while to understand.

No matter how lost or broken someone is, it is never too late to turn toward God. We can never give up hope. We can never stop praying. Moms are not perfect. We make mistakes. God knows I did, and He has forgiven me, my son has forgiven me, and I needed to forgive myself. There comes a time when being a mom is the most painful thing imaginable. I know. And that is when our prayers take on a life of their own.

And so, fellow moms, rest assured that God is in control. Through the pain and pleasure of motherhood, He is there to give us wisdom and guidance when we feel ignorant and lost. He is also there to rejoice with us when our children make choices that make Him happy and us proud, and He deserves our prayers of thanksgiving and praise, as well as those of pain and petition.

May *God Answers Moms' Prayers* bring you as much comfort and joy as it has brought me in its making. I pray your heart will be touched by His love.

God bless you.

Allison Bottke

1
Hopes and Dreams

THERE IS NOTHING WE CAN IMAGINE that is beyond God's ability to create. Every idea, hope, dream, or desire that He gives, He can bring to fruition. David sang in Psalm 16 of how he blesses the Lord "who counsels me" and relies on God to "make known to me the path of life." When something is so close to your heart, it can often seem impossible or become so important that God may ask you to place it on the altar. But as Isaac was redeemed at the last minute in a miraculous manner, our dreams, desires, and goals can also be fulfilled in His way, in His time, for "in Your right hand there are pleasures forever" (NASB).

Be strong and take heart, all you who hope in the LORD.

PSALM 31:24

As we grow older, some memories carry both poignant and painful recollections. We pray the "if only I could go back" prayer or the "if only I had done this" prayer. We usually pray with the realization that God is hearing our request, but we know He can never really give us back what has been lost, what time has taken away. Yet for Patricia, that was not really true.

᠊᠊ A Birthday Present from God ᠊᠊

BY PATRICIA SHEETS, VIRGINIA BEACH, VIRGINIA

God constantly and wonderfully amazes me. It seems the more I know of Him, the more I want to know. Just when I think I can predict what He is going to do next—*wham!*—He surprises me yet again. His latest surprise was the gift He gave me on my fiftieth birthday.

A few days before my birthday, I jokingly asked God for a birthday present. I asked to be a teenager again. As soon as I had spoken the prayer, a smile crept to my face. Even though I know God is all-powerful, I could not fathom how even He could make me a teenager again. I dismissed the prayer in my mind, got up, and went about my day, not once considering the possibility that God would answer this particular request.

Later that day, I received a frantic phone call from Heather, one of the teenagers in our church youth group. For some reason, this young lady has taken to me and assumes that I am her ally in the never-ending stream of circumstances in which she finds herself.

Her most recent crisis involved an argument with her mother and being grounded "for the rest of my life!" and not being able to talk on the phone with her boyfriend. I listened patiently as she told her woeful story, hoping she would release some pressure and gain composure. Instead she talked herself into a deeper frenzy and declared, "I hate my mom! I hope she never speaks to me again!"

As a mom and a Christian, I felt it was my duty to say something. I decided to tell a story from my own teenage years about one of the trials and tribulations I went through with my own mom.

Like most moms she had her very own list of finely tuned methods for harassing children. To awaken us each morning, instead of setting an alarm or dousing us with cold water, she would come into our rooms, happy and cheerful, and in a singsong voice that would put Julie Andrews to shame, sing, "Up, up, up! It's time to get up!" I don't remember exactly when this abuse began, but it became intolerable at about age 15. Every morning I would put the pillow over my head in an attempt to drown the words, but she continued her morning ritual until I could take it no longer.

When I finally got married and moved from my parents' home, I was thrilled that I would finally be free of what became known as "The Get-Up Song." I married an Army man and moved away, but on the morning of my twenty-first birthday, the phone rang and on the other end was a cheerful voice singing, "Up, up, up! It's time to get up!" Not even the United States military could stop her!

I lived with this annoyance every year of my life until two years ago. On the morning of my forty-eighth birthday, the phone call from my mom came later than normal. I was beginning to wonder if perhaps she had forgotten my birthday, but finally the call came and a tired, faint voice whispered "The Get-Up Song." I listened as tears streamed down my face. When she finished the song, I said, "Mom, can you sing it for me once more?" As she struggled through the melody one more time, I tried with all that was within me to capture and memorize the sound of the words I somehow felt would never pass her lips again.

"Heather," I said, "I am about to turn 50 in a few days. You can't imagine what it would mean to me to have the phone ring and hear those annoying, horrible words spoken again. I would give anything to have my mom back."

She seemed to gain some insight from my story and promised to try to work things out with her mom. I ended the conversation, thinking this was the last I would hear on the subject.

Early on the morning of my fiftieth birthday, the phone rang. I was startled, thinking someone had been in an accident, and quickly picked up the receiver. On the other end, a 16-year-old voice sang, "Up, up, up! It's time to get up!" Sweet, precious Heather. For one moment I was a kid again, 15 years old, without a care in the world except an annoying mother who sang silly songs.

Once again the Lord had performed a miracle. Once again He had come through for me, making me a teenager again, even for a brief moment in time. As I hung up the phone, I looked toward heaven and said, "Thank You, Lord, for the wonderful birthday present. Thank You for the memory of my mom, and thank You for sending me a teenager to help me feel like one again."

Looking out for our children is a priority in a mom's life. When times are rough and finances slim, no prayer is too difficult for the Lord to answer. Vickie prayed earnestly for one of her boys, and the Lord came through, just like she knew He would.

✌ *Just a Pair of Sunday Shoes* ✌

BY VICKIE PAPE, MORGANTOWN, KENTUCKY

I thought some things were just too trivial to pray about, but I learned that God cares about the little things, too.

When I was a young mother, I had four very small children. Sundays were difficult for me. Getting four little ones dressed for church was challenging. "We have to look our best to go to Jesus' house," I told each one as I helped them dress in their best clothes.

One of my sons, James, was especially concerned about looking his best. He was very responsible and would get all his things ready the night before without any reminder. Every Saturday he would polish his shoes and set out the outfit he was going to wear to church the next day.

James was so concerned about looking his best that he even worried about his tie. "I want a real tie," he would say whenever I tried to give him a clip-on one.

Church clothes don't often wear out, but boys frequently outgrow them, and James had done just that with his Sunday shoes. One day he came to me, shoes in hand. "Mom, my church shoes hurt my feet. I think I need some bigger ones."

That particular summer my husband had been laid off. We were struggling financially, and it was difficult to keep our growing children in clothes and shoes. There was no money in the budget for new shoes. We could not even pay our bills. It seemed we were falling farther behind each month. James was a practical boy, and I knew he would not have asked for shoes unless he really needed them.

"I'll see if I can find a pair at the thrift store or a garage sale. Can you wear them this week?" I asked.

"Yes, they only hurt my toes," he told me with a sweet smile.

"Okay, we'll look really hard this next week," I promised.

I did look hard. I went to every thrift store and garage sale I could find. I thought for sure I would be able to find something. It was just a pair of shoes. At each stop, though, I found only disappointment.

Each time I came home he would ask me, "Did you find any shoes for me, Mom?"

"No, honey," I would say, trying to sound hopeful. "But we'll keep looking."

Saturday night he came to me, asking, "What am I going to wear to church tomorrow?" his face wrinkled with concern. I felt so bad that I was unable to give him what he needed. It was just a pair of shoes, but it was so important to *him*. "Maybe you could wear your tennis shoes," I suggested. His tennis shoes were not in good shape, because they had already been through a whole year of school.

"Oh, Mom, those aren't nice. I don't want to wear them to Jesus' house," he said, looking very disappointed.

I knew he was right, but I didn't know what to do. I felt so helpless.

The next day we were all getting ready for church when James came out with his church shoes on. He looked like he was walking on nails. I could tell every step was painful for him. I didn't say anything, but my heart was pained for him.

At Sunday services the pastor talked about how God loves each of us and answers all our prayers. There was nothing too small to pray about. The pastor quoted James 5:16: "The prayer of a righteous man is powerful and effective."

It occurred to me that we had not yet prayed for shoes. I had never thought about praying for something so trivial before. It was just a pair of shoes. Then the thought came to my mind that it was not trivial to James.

That night I gathered my children around and told them we needed to say a prayer so we would be able to find some church shoes for James. I thanked God for all the blessings we did have, and then asked Him to help us find some church shoes for James this week.

I tucked the children into bed and, before I went to sleep, I prayed again about the shoes. I felt peaceful. A strong feeling touched my heart that God loves us and cares about the little things, too.

The next day was a typical cooking and cleaning day. While I was busy doing laundry, the phone rang. It was my friend Cathy, whom I had not talked to in quite a while.

"I was cleaning out my closets," she said, "and I have several boxes of clothes and things that are too small for my son. Will you be home later today so I can bring them over?"

"Yes!" I was excited to hear from her. "We would love to see you."

After I hung up the phone, I had an overwhelming sense that I would find a pair of Sunday shoes for James among the things Cathy was bringing over.

When Cathy got there, I went out to meet her and help her with the boxes. Sitting on top of one of the boxes was a pair of black dress shoes—"church shoes," as we called them. They looked to be just James's size.

I fought back the tears, I was so overwhelmed with love and gratitude to God. I knew He loved my family and was taking care of us through my friend.

We took the boxes in the house, and James tried on the shoes. They fit perfectly. He paraded around the front room showing them off. I told Cathy about our prayers and how she had brought the answer to them. She was thrilled to have had a part in our answered prayer.

It's amazing how much joy such a little thing can bring. But we learned that the little things do matter to God, even if it's just a pair of Sunday shoes.

We may say a prayer for something in our lives that needs an immediate answer. Yet sometimes when the answer comes, it is nothing like we thought and seems totally wrong. But in the end we find out God was right all along! For Sheila, a mistake turned out to be a miracle.

⌒ A Divine Misprint ⌒

BY SHEILA COREY, CLAYTON, INDIANA

It was our fourth move in seven years of ministry, and even in a congregation of 350 members, a new wave of loneliness swept over me. One morning as I dressed my two preschool children, a thought came to me and I got on my knees to pray. "God, I'm lonely. Send me someone who is lonely and needs a friend, too." I then began to scour the church directory in search of a woman with children who might want to get together for the day. After many unsuccessful attempts, I dialed the number next to a familiar name. A woman answered.

"Cheryl?" I asked.

"Yes?"

"This is Sheila from church. How are you?"

"Uh, I'm fine," she replied.

"How are the kids?"

"They're okay. A little wild today."

"Well, I'm calling because I'm taking my kids to the pool today and wanted to know if you could join me."

There was an awkward silence, and then reluctantly she said, "Okay."

I asked for directions to her house and was surprised to find she lived on the same road as we did, just a couple of miles east of our block. She came out of the house when I pulled into her driveway, and I soon discovered that the woman I was picking up was not the woman I thought I had called! I put on my Sunday face and welcomed her as if she was an old friend. I was, after all, a minister's wife, and thought she probably knew me. As we drove along, we talked about the church. She asked if I had met a particular church member yet, and I said, "No." I asked if she knew another church member, and she said, "No." In the course of the conversation, we eventually realized we were from two different congregations.

She asked how I got her number, and I told her about my search through the church directory. We discovered that she shared the same first name as the lady I intended to call, and that her telephone number appeared in the directory by mistake. Amazed, I told her of my prayer that morning. When I finished, she said through her tears, "God answered your prayer. My husband told me recently that he had an affair. I don't know who to turn to. I truly do need a friend today."

Cheryl and I spent the day talking, crying, and at times even laughing with amazement at God's way of putting two needy women together. After dropping her off at the end of the day, I went home, immediately opened the directory, and called her.

"Cheryl?"

She laughed and then replied, "Yes?"

"Just checking to see if you were real."

"I guess our friendship really was made in heaven," was her chuckling reply.

"Amen to that, my new sister. Amen to that."

The church directory was printed a year before my husband and I arrived at our new church. God scheduled my moment with Cheryl through a misprint. He knew Cheryl's need a year before she did! He knew, even in my loneliness, that He could use me. I learned that day, as did Cheryl, that God knows the needs of His people. If we are available to Him, no matter what our circumstances, He will use us to meet those needs.

> Moms the world over have prayed for a "few minutes of peace and quiet." We long for a time just to rest up and be able to face another day of "mommyhood." Paula put her faith in God and offered up her prayers into God's hands, asking Him for a special time of refreshment, and He did not let her down.

A Blizzard, A Baby, and a Swimming Pool

BY PAULA MOLDENHAUER, THORNTON, COLORADO

Child number four was a surprise. It put me off balance when I first took the home pregnancy test. I cried a little, stomped around, and rushed to my doctor to confirm the pregnancy. When I called my husband, he said, "You're kidding, right?" But by the end of the day when I asked him how he felt, he said, "Happy."

And I said, "Me, too."

Our acceptance and joy over the thought of another child did not change the facts. We already had three children, five and under, and the littlest was only nine months old. The birth of our fourth child would mean another whirlwind of nursing and sleepless nights, and our third was not yet weaned! Tired and weary, I began asking God for some special time alone with my husband before the baby came. It seemed with the demands of our young children that we didn't get much time alone to nurture our marriage, and I knew another baby would only exacerbate that fact. I longed to be held, to talk without interruption, and to focus on the love that had brought us together. Our need for togetherness often got shoved aside as we focused on parenthood.

When my husband was invited to participate in a focus group at an insurance company's national convention, and I was invited to join him for an all-expense-paid trip to a five-star resort, I believed God had answered my prayer.

My doctor told me he could not condone a trip to Arizona two weeks before my due date, but I made the airline reservation, convinced that our three-day getaway was a gift from my heavenly Father and all would be well. I hummed as I lined up babysitters for the other children.

We were scheduled to fly out in two days when it hit. It will be remembered as the blizzard of '96. The airport was shut down. No one flew in or out. The vendors could not support the need for food for stranded travelers. Transportation even to the nearby hotels was impossible.

The snow piled higher than our first-floor windows, and I fretted as I packed my suitcase, hoping the roads could be cleared in time for us to leave.

The first day the airport was operational was the day my husband and I were to fly out. Convinced God had given us this time, I waddled down the long corridors of the airport, trying to ignore the swelling crowds and repeated announcements of canceled flights.

We reached our gate only to discover that our flight, too, had been canceled. My courage waned. We were directed to the main terminal for flight reassignment, and I limped toward the escalator with a sinking feeling. I did not want to let go of my dream of time alone with Jerry! My husband kissed my cheek and whispered, "You told me this is from God. If it's His gift, don't you think we'll get to go?"

The happy ending to the story is that we miraculously made it on one of two flights that left for Phoenix. Hardly anyone flew out that day, but we did.

The first thing my husband said when we walked into our amazing hotel room was, "Oh, honey! I would be miserable here without you." He grabbed me in his arms and twirled me around, protruding belly and all.

We spent our mini-vacation in surroundings unlike anything either of us had ever experienced: a sunken tub in our 450-dollar-per-night room, plush robes, breakfast from room service, and pristine swimming pools where I simply raised a flag for my every need to be attended—all courtesy of my husband's company.

We took leisurely walks in the resort garden, lingered over meals prepared by top-ranking chefs, and swam. I will never forget the luscious red raspberries eaten next to a fancy pool or the best tortilla soup I have ever tasted. But the fancy surroundings and new, luxurious experiences were only a backdrop to the best part: long, intimate conversations and time to simply be alone and focus on each other.

Less than two weeks after we returned home, our precious baby, Samuel Paul, arrived and his three older siblings clustered around him in amazement. My husband and I entered another round of diapers, midnight feedings, and weariness buoyed up by God's romantic getaway for two.

I will never forget how God answered the prayers of this tired mommy. He took us through the blizzard of the decade to a warm, dry place, and we swam in the luxurious waters of His love.

How many times have you prayed for something you simply "know" God will grant you? How many times is that something only part of what you really want? Kathleen found, with the help of two strangers, how to "pray the impossible" for her son.

∽ *Pray the Impossible* ∼

BY KATHLEEN SZITAS, GREENSBORO, NORTH CAROLINA

"Just focus on finishing the best you can," I said as I finished bandaging my 15-year-old son's blistered foot. I smiled despite the torment inside me.

The heat index was over 100 degrees, Steven's blisters looked like extra toes, yet this was the cross-country meet wherein he hoped to break his 30-minute time streak. How was that possible? I had watched Steven struggle with the decision just a few weeks ago to join the cross-country team.

"I can't run like the other boys," he had blurted out. "I'll make a fool of myself."

I was rocked to the core. Even when the doctors told us when he was just ten years old that he might never walk again after complications from a surgery to correct a birth defect on his right leg, Steven had never given up. Not only did he walk again, he also endured several more painful surgeries, astounding everyone, including his doctors, with his determination and spirit. We had placed him in God's hands, yet at times I had a hard time letting go.

Deep inside, I had my doubts about his ability to run cross-country, but I kept silent and prayed. In the end, Steven joined the team. He ran his first 3.1-mile race in 32:48 minutes. He finished his next race in a little over 30 minutes. Over the next several meets, he kept a steady 30-minute time. To watch him sprint across the finish line literally took my breath away. No one would ever know that his right leg was smaller, weaker, and bore deep scars from his many surgeries. Yet discouragement set in.

"I can't do this," he said one night. "I can't get under 30 minutes. I always come in last! I said I couldn't do this, but no one would listen." I couldn't find words to comfort him because my own heart was crowded with doubt.

As I rushed through my hectic schedule that day, my thoughts raced with anxiety and disjointed prayer. Was running cross-country a mistake? What if he really could not run as fast as the other boys? How would he handle it if, once again, he came in last? Should I keep encouraging him, or should I just back off? Yet over and over I prayed for a "29" for Steven. Just one minute from his time, I knew, would relight the fire in his spirit.

"Stay close to him, Lord," I whispered as I watched Steven walk off and join his team.

"Kathie, do you have Sean with you?" The sound of the coach's voice startled me. I always brought my nine-year-old son with me to the events. I smiled as I recalled the answer to an unspoken prayer when, at the last minute, a neighbor had offered to keep Sean while I came to the meet. Sean would not have lasted five minutes in this heat.

"No, not today," I answered.

"Good. I have a job for you. Follow him," the coach said as he pointed to the assistant coach.

I found myself walking away from the starting line, and even further from the points along the 3.1-mile route where I would cheer Steven on. My heart sank deeper with each step. Finally we stopped.

"Stay here and direct the runners this way," the coach directed as he pointed to a steep path almost hidden among the trees. He explained that the runners would come by twice, and only on the second time around would I need to direct them.

Before I could utter a word, he was gone. I stood in the middle of the woods with mosquitoes buzzing around my head and sweat dripping down my cheeks—just one more piece of darkness to add to my dimming spirit. I could not believe I was not going to see Steven run this crucial race. I spotted a small wooden bridge several feet away and went over and plopped down on its rail. I blinked back my tears and soon felt the need to pray rise up in me like a swelling tide. Suddenly I heard voices.

"Hi there," a thin, gray-haired man called out with a wave of his hand. His other hand clasped the hand of a white-haired lady I assumed was his wife. Their smiles were warm and inviting as I explained why I was there. As we continued to talk, I felt like I was among old friends. I will never forget the moment when the spunky old man exclaimed he was a Christian and had been for 35 years.

"I'm a Christian, too," I said, feeling a flood of warmth that had nothing to do with the temperature of the day. "I was just getting ready to pray when you came along. I can't believe I have to be here instead of watching my son run, but I haven't had a moment of quiet time lately, so I thought I would pray while I waited." I could not believe I was gushing out all this to complete strangers.

"Pray the impossible!" the man boomed.

I almost toppled off my perch.

"Do you know Mark 11:24?" he asked excitedly. He didn't wait for a reply.

"Whatever you ask for in prayer, believe that you have received it, and it will be yours."

"Yes! I know that Scripture!" I said.

His wife was smiling ear to ear, and I had to resist the urge to hug them both. Then I spotted runners coming. This was their first time around, so I stayed put and cheered them on. Then came Steven. I leapt off the rail and started cheering louder.

"That's my son," I said. My eyes burned with joyful tears.

"He's limping," the woman stated quietly.

I was still looking in the direction of where Steven had run. "When he gets tired, his limp gets more pronounced, " I said, almost to myself.

"Why does he limp?" the man asked.

It was a simple question, but did not come with a simple answer. I drew in a deep breath and explained about Steven's leg. When I was through there was silence, and for a moment I wished I had not said anything.

"Have you ever asked God to restore his leg?"

I opened my mouth to answer, but nothing came out. No one had ever asked me that before.

"Pray the impossible," he said again. "We pray for what we think can happen, what we think is possible, but nothing is impossible with God."

I was awestruck. But the sound of more runners jolted me back. It was time for me to do my job! As I directed the runners, I glanced back to my new friends who stood watching me. I longed to get back to them.

"We've got to go now, Missy," I heard the man call out after a while. It dawned on me when he called me Missy that we did not even know each other's names! I waved good-bye, sad to see them go. Then I saw a lone runner coming my way.

"I'm okay, I'm okay," Steven chanted as he passed me and turned up the path.

I couldn't hold back my tears. He did look okay, despite the heat, the blisters, and the turmoil in his spirit! Suddenly the man's words hit me. Pray the impossible! We pray what we think can happen. Isn't that what I had been doing, praying what I thought possible? But nothing is impossible with God. This truth hit me hard, and I felt awash with excitement. Bursts of cheers startled me. The runners must be coming in to finish. I had to get to Steven. Not seeing any more runners coming, I took off, my mind still racing.

Running a 29-minute race is what I believed possible for Steven. Where was my faith? What if God had more in store for Steven today than I could even imagine? Hadn't God showed me time and time again He was the God of the impossible? Hadn't I placed Steven in His hands long ago?

Lean not on your own understanding. The piece of Scripture came into my heart. I had, in fact, been leaning only on my understanding.

"Lord," I cried in between gasps for breath, "forgive me." I felt peace flood through me, chasing away all my doubts and darkness. My legs burned from exhaustion, but my heart was soaring. I reached the finish line and saw Steven walking toward me. I bent over to catch my breath.

"Mom."

Something in the way he spoke startled me, and I stood up.

"I ran a 27."

I fell to my knees and wept with joy. It was more than I could ever have imagined. God sent me those two angels that day to renew my faith and change my prayer life forever. "Pray the impossible" has become a constant reminder in my life to lean on God and not my own understanding. Steven finished the season with a 24:10-minute time. He is now in his second season on the cross-country team.

Have you ever prayed for something, and the Lord's response gave you more than one choice? Did you debate on which one to choose, feeling deep in your heart that only one was the right choice? Sandra had this decision to make after one such prayer to the Lord.

∽: *However the Lord Leads* :∽

BY SANDRA MCGARRITY, CHESAPEAKE, VIRGINIA

I opened the front door, hoping to catch a breeze in the already-steaming Florida morning. I noticed that a flyer was tucked into the handle of the screen door. I removed the flyer and saw that it was from the local meat market. I couldn't resist taking a peek inside. As usual, the small store had a great sale going on. Oh well, it didn't matter. Even if meat were on sale for a nickel a pound, I wouldn't be going shopping that day.

With the flyer still in my hand, I took my Bible to the couch, hoping for some quiet time before my two little daughters woke up. I read some Scripture and then began the usual round of prayers for friends and family. I moved on to prayer for our needs. With my husband in Bible college, there were always material needs to pray for. I remembered the flyer and took another look at it.

"Lord, my family hasn't had meat in several weeks. This is such a good sale. If I had just ten dollars, I could buy enough meat to feed us for two or more weeks. I'm asking You to make a way for me to buy some of this meat." As my prayer ended, my mouth fairly watered at the thought of a juicy hamburger.

I went about the morning's business of feeding and dressing my daughters. When they were settled in, I began the housework. A few hours later, I heard the tread of the postal carrier on the front porch. I went to retrieve the mail and settled into the old glider to read it.

There was the usual junk mail, but also a letter from the wife of a former pastor at our church.

The first thing I noticed was that a check was tucked in with the letter. After some news about her family and the church, she explained the check. She said the money was for me and that she wanted me to buy some fabric to make a new dress. My heart leapt into my throat in excitement. New dresses were few and far between. The letter continued, "or however the Lord leads." The word *however* was underlined three times.

An uneasy feeling came over me as I thought about the type of fabric I could buy. The word *however* kept invading my thoughts. I tried to reason my way through the situation. She had said the money was for fabric. That was her intent. Why shouldn't I use the money for what she had sent it for? I needed a new dress. Why shouldn't I have a new dress? Why did she have to add the words "however the Lord leads"? Why didn't she just say, "Buy some fabric"? Why did I have to go and pray for money for meat that morning?

That was the bottom line. I had prayed for money to buy meat for my family. She had said that I was to spend the money "however the Lord leads." The *however* had been underlined three times. I had not prayed for money to buy fabric. If she had simply instructed me to buy fabric, I would have, but she had not. I could almost feel the new dress being pulled from my hands.

I knew what I had to do. I got my purse and car keys. "Come on, girls! We're going to the meat market!"

At the meat market I bought a couple of chickens, a huge pack of ground beef, and 18 eggs. Back at home, I wrapped the meat into individual packages and put them in the freezer. It was exciting to see all of that meat tucked away for our use over the weeks to come— almost as exciting as a new dress. I fed lunch to my daughters and put them down for a nap. I made my way to the glider on the porch, hoping to catch a breeze in the afternoon heat.

At peace with my decision, I thanked the Lord for His provision and confessed that I would never have been at peace with buying fabric. I asked Him to help me to not be selfish, and I just sat there for a while enjoying the quiet of the late afternoon.

I saw my neighbor coming across the lawn between our two houses. Her husband was also a student at the Bible college and our lifestyles were very similar. I noticed as I called out a greeting that she had something draped across her arm. It appeared to be clothing of some sort. She must want my opinion about something, or maybe she needed my help with mending.

"Hi," she said. "Brenda made this lovely dress, and it turned out too small for her, so she gave it to me."

Lucky you, I thought, waiting to see what kind of help she needed.

"The dress doesn't fit me, either, but I think it might be just right for you." She held out the dress as my jaw dropped.

In amazement, I told her about the money I had received that morning.

"Well then, this dress is most definitely for you," she answered.

I hurried into the house to try the dress on. It was made in the latest style. It was my favorite color, blue, and of course it fit perfectly!

I wore that dress until it was practically worn out. Even then I hated to part with it. After it was no longer wearable, I incorporated some of the fabric into a quilt. The memory of that dress will always live on in my heart as a lesson of God's faithfulness to His children.

"Now to him who is able to do immeasurably more than all we ask or imagine, according to his power that is at work within us, to him be glory in the church and in Christ Jesus throughout all generations, for ever and ever! Amen" (Ephesians 3:20-21).

Lois and Leonard Swenson never realized that taking in a small child would someday turn out to be the answer to one of their prayers. A prayer for their very own daughter.

⌁ *Prayer for Gideon's Bride* ⌁

BY MURIEL LARSON, GREENVILLE, SOUTH CAROLINA

"When you came to our tribe to tell us about Jesus, I learned of your home for boys." A gaunt-looking nomad mother stood before missionaries Lois and Leonard Swenson. "My husband is blind, and I must work in the fields all day and cannot take care of our little boy. Will you take him into your home?"

Lois looked down on the small boy with matted hair and big brown eyes. Then she looked at her husband. "I know we don't usually take in boys with two living parents, Leonard, but this is a special case."

Leonard nodded and smiled at the little boy's mother. "Yes, we'll take him in."

Little did they know what an amazing part this little Arab boy, Mohammed El Hamoud, would someday play in their lives.

After the young boy's mother left, Lois removed the filthy rags Mohammed was wearing and threw them away. Leonard shaved the boy's head and made sure he had a shower. They clothed him in clean pajamas and put him in a clean bed.

The next morning, they found him on the floor. He was not used to sleeping in a bed, and it took him weeks to adjust to this strange custom.

Mohammed started school right away, and Leonard and Lois found him to be a very obedient child, as well as a good student. He adjusted quickly to the orphanage procedures and became good friends with the Swensons' seven-year-old son, Daniel. The boys often included Dan's younger sister, Becky, in their games.

As time passed, Mohammed listened closely to the orphanage teachers. He learned God's Word, memorized Scripture, and sang gospel songs with the rest of the children. When he was nine years old, he accepted Jesus as his Lord and Savior.

"I am a Christian now and I love Jesus," he told Leonard one day. "I do not want to be called Mohammed anymore. I am no longer Moslem, so I want to be called 'Gideon.'"

Each boy in the orphanage was sponsored by Christians in more affluent countries, and Gideon's sponsor, a vice president of a large company in the United States, enabled Gideon to attend high school in Beirut and then at an Armenian college.

One of Gideon's professors encouraged Gideon to continue his education in America. So again, with his sponsor's support, Gideon graduated from college in the United States with a degree in math. Upon graduation, his faithful sponsor even helped him find a job.

Meanwhile, Becky, Dan's sister, another of Gideon's childhood friends, was in America, too, working on her nursing degree. In fact, Gideon, or "Jed" as he was affectionately called, often joined Dan and Becky at holiday gatherings with family.

Once Gideon was securely settled in a home of his own, he found four of his orphanage "brothers" and let them stay with him until they found jobs and homes of their own. Becky often joined them on weekends and helped them clean house or prepare meals.

One night Becky could tell that something was troubling Gideon. "What's wrong, Jed?"

He looked up at her from the other side of the room. "Becky, I love you."

Becky was stunned. "Well, Jed, I love you, too, but I am not in love with you, and there is a difference—a big difference."

Gideon was heartbroken.

What he did not know was that the Swensons had always prayed for their children's future mates. Gideon, as well as Becky, was included in that prayer.

Several months later, Becky called her parents to tell them she had a few days off and was going to Denver to visit with some friends. "Jed's going to meet me there, too."

It never surprised Leonard and Lois to hear that Becky was getting together with Gideon. Their relationship had continued from the time they were eight and six years old.

Several nights later, the Swensons' phone rang. "Hello? Becky, hi. Oh, and Jed, how are you both? Is everything okay? It's awfully late to be calling." Leonard's voice took on a more serious tone. "You're old enough to make those decisions on your own, Gideon, and you, too, Becky."

Lois bolted out of bed. "What's going on?"

"Jed and Becky want to talk with you, Lois." Leonard handed her the phone.

"Did you hear the good news, Mom?" Becky sounded positively giddy.

Then Jed chimed in. "Mom, we want to get married!"

"Married?" The news stunned Lois. "I never thought about you two...well, I always thought of you as brother and sister," she stammered.

"Jed and I love each other, Mom. Actually, he told me he loved me several months ago. I was as surprised as you are now, but I prayed about it and I am confident that he is God's choice for me."

During the wedding ceremony, before Becky walked down the aisle, Gideon shared his story. "I remember the Swensons' first trip to my Bedouin tribe when I was six years old. I remember seeing Dan and Becky walking around the camp. I had never seen blond children before, and I asked my mother what they were. She told me they were children just like me, but from another country. I knew from the moment I laid eyes on Becky that I loved her, and I have loved her ever since."

Lois and Leonard could hardly contain the joy they were feeling. In one day, prayers for two of their children were answered. Gideon's bride was God's choice, and their prayer for Becky's husband was answered at the same moment.

2

Baby Blessings

I<small>T'S LIKE A SPECIAL CLUB: MOTHERHOOD</small>. And it's truly gender specific, to say the least. What a gift the Father has given to His daughters, to allow us to bear and nurture children! And through the miracle of adoption, even women who cannot give birth can still know the tenacious love of a child in their keeping. What heartbreaking pain we can suffer and what inconceivable joy we can have, all because we are mothers. Yet in reality we are merely caretakers, very attached to our work. Our children are on loan from God and entrusted to our safekeeping for as long as He deems right. We find the direction and guidance needed when we turn them over to Him. He knows each child intimately, ever since He began knitting each one together in the womb. Yes, motherhood is a very special club. And it's an honor to be invited by God to join.

*Sons are a heritage from the L*ORD*, children a reward from him.*

<small>PSALM 127:3</small>

Losing a much-prayed-for child before it is even born can make even the strongest woman falter in her faith. Martha never lost hope in her prayer for a child. And the Lord provided abundantly!

⌁ Beside Still Waters ⌁

BY MARTHA BOLTON, NASHVILLE, TENNESSEE

Someone once said, "Experience is what you get when you don't get what you want."

Plans fall apart, people let us down, our hopes and expectations do not come to pass, and life takes an unexpected turn. We get experience.

Less than a year after suffering a miscarriage 12 weeks into my pregnancy, I discovered I was pregnant again. This time the pregnancy went along smoothly. Friends and family gave me three baby showers. We painted and wallpapered the nursery in anticipation of the new arrival.

About one week from my due date, my obstetrician failed to pick up the baby's heartbeat on the monitor. I tried to convince myself nothing was wrong. The baby was simply positioned in such a way that we could not hear the heartbeat.

The doctor sent my husband and me home, stating that if no heartbeat was detected at my next appointment, labor would need to be induced.

That night I prayed to God to let me feel something—the slightest movement, anything—to let me know the baby was going to be all right. But all I felt was stillness.

The next morning, plans were finalized for labor to be induced that very day. My medical doctor believed waiting longer could be dangerous for me if the baby had died.

My husband, Russ, drove me to the hospital, but it was not the same frantic drive we had rehearsed so many times. There was little excitement and even less conversation. We were both too busy praying to God to give us the strength to make it through this, no matter what He had decided for our unborn child.

Labor was induced, and for the rest of the day and into the night we listened to the silence of the monitor. The pain that silence brought was worse than the contractions.

In the early-morning hours, after what seemed an eternity of hoping against hope, I delivered a ten-pound, two-ounce stillborn son.

We named the baby Hugh Leon after both grandfathers, and although we never got the chance to hold our son, we took comfort in knowing in whose arms he was now resting.

It wasn't easy walking by the nursery night after night, seeing the empty crib and silent toys, but my husband and I never gave up praying that the Lord would someday bless us with a family.

We had always talked about adopting children in addition to any we might have. We began applying at every adoption agency we could find. We soon discovered that most of the adoption agencies had waiting lists longer than the Congressional Record. There was nothing for us to do but add our names, wait, and pray.

I filled my time now with writing and directing plays and comedy sketches for several congregations in our area. Russ busied himself with his work and leading a Scouting program at our church.

After several years of waiting and hoping, the Lord led us to take a giant step of faith. We sold our memory-filled two-bedroom home and bought a four-bedroom one.

Our friends lovingly commented that we were nuts. Why would we buy a house that big when we didn't have any children? We didn't...now. But we were praying that one day God would help us fill up those bedrooms with the happy laughter of our children. It was just a matter of time.

Unfortunately we soon found out it was a matter of zip code, too.

When I telephoned the adoption agencies to give them our new address, several of them informed me we could no longer be on their adoption list since we were no longer in the same county. We were stunned. Were we going to have to start all over again? Had our giant step of faith turned into a giant step backward?

Our church was having special services all that week, but I didn't feel like going to any of them. I was in no mood to listen to stories about how much God loved me.

Instead of going to church, my husband and I decided to stay home and continue unpacking. We had been in our new home one week and were still in wall-to-wall boxes. Figuring it would be the easiest room to arrange, we decided to start in the nursery.

We hung baby clothes, moved furniture around, and nailed up wall decorations. It seemed a bit futile to spend so much time arranging a room that was not being used, but the Lord seemed to be driving us to finish.

Russ was driven until about midnight. He had to go to work early the next day, so I stayed up to complete the job, even though I ended up doing more crying than unpacking.

It wasn't fair. None of this was fair. We had heard the news reports of abandoned babies being found in trash bins. Here we had everything for a baby, and plenty of love, yet the crib remained empty.

After a few more hours of licking my wounds and being mad at God, I finally surrendered. God had already proved His love by giving His only Son to die on the cross. If He never did another thing for me, that was enough. Who was I to ask for more? I didn't understand why any of this was happening in our lives, but in spite of it all, I vowed to continue serving Him. I prayed for His forgiveness of my anger and frustration. If it was His will, children would fill the rooms in our home when He was ready.

I dried my tears, finished the room at about 2:00 AM, and went to bed.

At 6:00 AM, the telephone rang. One of the out-of-state adoption agencies where we had applied had a baby boy waiting for us, barely three weeks old! Four hours after I had given the matter over to God and ceased trying to make things work by myself, the Lord answered our prayers.

I was on the earliest flight I could get, too excited to worry about my fear of flying. Talk about an emotional high. The plane was cruising at an altitude of 30,000 feet; I was cruising at 35,000!

The agency worker met me at the airport and handed me the greatest belated Mother's Day gift I could have prayed for. We named him Russ after my husband. And Russ was just the beginning of God's blessings. Almost two years later we adopted two-day-old Matt. Three and a half months after Matt came into our lives, I gave birth to our third son, Tony Shane.

Once we gave the matter over to God, praying for His will to be done, He had taken over. Our four-bedroom step of faith turned out to be a step forward after all. In just two short years, God had filled every bedroom!

How does a mom handle her own child's announcement of an unexpected pregnancy? Pat prayed the Lord would show them what to do, and He provided far beyond anything she could have ever hoped or prayed for.

Angel Kisses

BY MARILYN NASETH, FARIBAULT, MINNESOTA (AS TOLD BY PAT DUNN)

"Angel kisses"—that's what I call the freckles on my grand-daughter's sweet angel face. When a new batch crops up, I count them for her. Our time together is precious. Often Cortney will say to me, "Grandma, tell me the story of my birth again."

In the fall of 1992, I was asked to teach the teen Sunday school class at my church. I decided to teach about some of the perils of being a teenager, focusing especially on abstinence. My 17-year-old son, Jason, was in my class.

A few weeks later Jason and Amanda, his girlfriend, stopped at my office. I am a nutrition and weight-loss counselor, which often involves discussing difficult situations in my clients' personal lives. I was no stranger to helping people sort out life challenges.

"What are you two doing here?" I asked, hugging them both.

Jason replied, "We want to talk to you, Mom, and after that can we get a chocolate malt on the way home?"

Jason had been telling me all week he wanted a chocolate malt. I teasingly said to him, "You've been craving a malt all week. Are you pregnant?"

Jason and Amanda exchanged nervous glances.

"Okay, kids, what's going on?"

I looked at Amanda and asked, "Amanda, are you pregnant?"

She quietly answered, "Yes," and my heart flip-flopped in my chest.

Amanda started to cry, and Jason just stood there, not knowing what to do or say. I gave them each a hug, saying, "Well, we've been through hard times before. We'll get through this, too. Amanda, are you sure you're pregnant?"

"Yes. Jason, my mom, and I just got back from the doctor's office. I am definitely pregnant."

Hesitantly, I questioned her again. "Do you believe in abortion?"

"No!" she said vehemently.

I breathed a huge sigh of relief. Then the professional side of me took over. "Okay, honey, how far along are you? What did the doctor say? Did he give you a prescription for prenatal vitamins? What do you plan to do?" My questions flowed nonstop.

My mind raced as I struggled to accept this reality. "Dear Lord," I prayed silently, "my son's 15-year-old girlfriend is pregnant. Please give me wisdom and strength to know what to say, to know what to do."

Amanda's parents were splitting up and were unable to give her the support she so desperately needed. Amanda had planned to keep the baby, but neither of her parents were willing to accept the responsibility of helping their daughter raise a child. Essentially homeless, Amanda moved in with us. When Amanda realized she was not prepared to raise this baby alone, she made the responsible decision to arrange plans for the baby's adoption.

Jason came to me one day and asked, "Mom, what about Julie and Bill? Do you think they would want to adopt our baby?"

Julie is my younger sister. She and her husband, Bill, had been trying to conceive a child for 15 years. Adopting Jason and Amanda's baby would be an answer to their prayers.

When I talked to Amanda about it, she was extremely opposed to the idea.

"No," she said firmly. "If I am not able to be involved in my baby's life, I don't think Jason should be either." She was in pain and I could understand, if not agree with, her feelings.

As Amanda's pregnancy progressed, my roller-coaster ride continued. I felt a mixture of excitement and sadness. This was my first grandchild, and I felt all the emotions of elation. But realistically, I knew I might never be able to watch my grandchild grow up.

"Dear Lord," I prayed, "please help find a solution to our problem. I would love to have my grandchild around and be involved. Please find a way for this to happen."

The adoption agency that Amanda and Jason were working with was not at all helpful. They became totally frustrated with the agency. In retrospect, I can now see how the Lord was orchestrating events along a different path.

My family pressured me to talk to Amanda again about Julie and Bill adopting her baby. How could I convince this young girl to change her mind? Should I even try? Was this the best way to go—having my sister and brother-in-law raise my grandchild? Or was I being selfish in wanting to keep the child near me? What was the best decision for the child? My emotions twisted and turned until I thought I would have a complete emotional breakdown. Prayer became my lifeline. "Lord, help me to be strong."

Although her own life was in turmoil, Amanda's mother stayed in touch with her daughter and tried to help her make a responsible decision. About six weeks before the baby was born, on Father's Day, Amanda called me into her room. "I have decided to let Julie and Bill adopt the baby." Just like that.

Excitedly I called my sister. "Julie, tell Bill 'Happy Father's Day.'"

My puzzled sister said, "What are you talking about?"

"Amanda has changed her mind. She wants you and Bill as the adoptive parents for her baby." Then Julie and I both screamed and cried together.

It seemed too good to be true. I worried that Amanda would change her mind and Bill and Julie would have their hopes dashed once again. They would be devastated to lose this chance for a baby of their own. "Please, dear Lord," I prayed fervently, "please do not let Amanda change her mind."

My family had a baby shower for Julie, padding her flat tummy with a pillow. I tried to join in the fun and excitement, but I was too numb. The stress of the past months and the thought of the upcoming birth pressed heavily on my spirit. I rejoiced with my sister, but grieved for my son and his girlfriend. I prayed this truly was the best decision. What if we were wrong?

Finally the day arrived when Amanda went into labor. She went to the hospital. Jason, her mother, and I rushed to join her. Over the next several hours, I watched my son cater to Amanda's needs, trying to make her comfortable. As she lashed out at him in pain and anger, he looked away in tears. Puzzled, he asked me, "Mom, why is Amanda being so hard on me?"

I tried to explain some of the emotions a woman in labor experiences. "Amanda knows she will soon be giving up her baby. This is very difficult for her. Hang in there, honey. It will be over shortly," I consoled him. I was very proud of my son, but my heart ached for him. It was his baby, too, and although the baby would remain in his family, he was giving up his rights as the father.

Cortney Amanda was born at 8:15 PM on August 2, weighing nine pounds, six ounces. Honoring Amanda's wishes, the baby was taken out of the room without Amanda seeing her newborn daughter. But Jason was right there. He was the first to notice the baby's mouth and chin were identical to his. He touched her little chin and looked at me with his heart in his eyes.

Then it was time to call the new parents. Julie and Bill were anxiously awaiting our call. My son hovered around the nursery, holding his little daughter as much as he could.

The next day Julie and Bill came to my office before going to the hospital. Julie was dressed in pink from head to toe. Together the three of us went to meet their new daughter. I prayed silently, "Thank You, God, for answering our prayers."

As we came around the corner in the hospital maternity ward, we spotted Jason seated in a chair, rocking the baby. He was holding her in front of him, as if to memorize her features. Even from a distance we could see that the baby's profile exactly matched that of her daddy. For me it was a heart-stopping moment.

Jason turned and smiled as we approached him. He stood and placed the baby in Julie's eager arms saying, "Congratulations, Mom and Dad. You have a beautiful baby daughter." I cried happy tears for Julie and Bill as I watched their radiant faces. I was proud of my son and of Amanda for putting the welfare of this tiny baby first.

Many times I have marveled at God's goodness and mercy in this situation. I have been able to be a full-fledged grandma to my precious Cortney, who is now 11 years old. This darling girl has enriched Julie and Bill's lives. Amanda's mom has also been a part of

Cortney's life. She is a much-loved child. Amanda herself chose to remain out of Cortney's life, allowing her to fully bond with Julie— a decision that while painful for Amanda, gave Cortney a balanced childhood.

Jason is now married to a strong, supportive woman, and they feel blessed to be the happy parents of a little girl—my second grandchild, Peyton.

Amanda, too, has another baby daughter to love and care for.

God took a difficult situation—a teenage pregnancy—to answer our prayers. Jason and Amanda's unselfish decision to give up their newborn baby was not arrived at lightly or easily. But it resulted in a joyful answer to prayer in the lives of my sister and her husband, who had waited 15 long years for a child. It was a decision that also allowed me, a proud and happy grandma, to give praise and thanksgiving to my Lord for hearing and answering the deepest prayers of my heart. Thank You, Jesus!

Some prayers are answered in minutes, some in days, some in weeks, and some in months. But Gloria and Rick's prayer took 21 years to be answered, coming full circle to where it began.

ᴗᴗ *Full-Circle Prayer* ᴗᴗ

BY GLORIA HELEN PLAISTED, KNIFE RIVER, MINNESOTA

One May morning as my husband, Rick, and I were preparing for the lunch rush in our restaurant, I answered the phone, expecting to take another order. The woman who called wasted no time in getting to the point. She said she was a social worker. "The daughter you gave up for adoption 22 years ago is seeking to find her biological parents."

I squeezed my eyes shut and opened them wide several times, thinking I was dreaming. "Could you repeat what you just said?" Perhaps I didn't hear her right. She kindly obliged. I dropped to my knees, and a cold shiver came over my body as I wept. The phone slipped out of my hand. Rick and I had waited 21 years, three months, and nine days for that phone call.

When I was nine years old, my mother died. It was a cataclysmic event that changed me forever. My mother left not only me behind, but also my six siblings. The three oldest marched into the military, and the younger ones went into foster homes. I was left alone with my father, who was a compulsive gambler and was rarely home. Practically speaking, I raised myself. I ate alone, went off to school alone, and came home to an empty house.

I met Rick when I was 14 years old. Both of us came from broken homes. Unfortunately neither of us had any hint of spiritual or moral guidance when we were young. Rick and I became physically intimate. I guess I thought our love would cover a multitude of problems. I may not have known then that sex outside of marriage was wrong, but I learned quickly it has a world of consequences.

At 16 I learned that I was pregnant. I knew I was too young to be a responsible mother. I could barely take care of myself, let alone a child. Rick and I both felt overwhelmed, but we knew we wanted more for our child than teenage parents could offer.

After nine months in Seton Center for Unwed Mothers, on September 16, 1969, I gave birth to Jennifer Lee, the most beautiful baby on earth. She loved us and we loved her, but as we worked through our emotions, we decided that love would not feed her or give her a future. We decided to give her up for adoption.

We tried to concentrate on the fact that many couples could not have children, and this beautiful child would be their miracle. We kissed her fuzzy cheeks, whispered in her ear, and prayed that one day we would be able to hold her again. As Rick and I snuggled with her for the last time, I felt as if my heart was being ripped in two.

I returned to high school in the spring and married Rick shortly after I graduated. As time went by, Rick and I "grew up" and started a restaurant business. We were thankful to become pregnant again with our son, but scared about whether we could do this parenting thing. What will we do when the baby starts to cry? Do I carry him or put him in the crib? Do you pin or tape a diaper? Although we both felt inadequate, we knew we were better equipped than when our daughter was born.

When we were in our thirties, our understanding of adoption took on a new, deeper meaning when we both accepted Jesus Christ as our Lord and Savior. We were now adopted into God's family. I realized my Father in heaven knows what it is like to lose a child. I was deeply moved.

Because adoption held such a special place in our hearts, we began praying for a child to adopt. Next we had to prove we were suitable parents. The screening process left no stone unturned. How did we handle anger? How were we parented? Amazingly, we were approved for placement of a child. Now it was time to wait, pray, and trust God to move in our favor.

Five years later we received the call. We were to pick up our 15-month-old daughter!

So many thoughts ran through my head on that drive to Wisconsin. *Would I be ready? Will she like us? How will our son feel?* My thoughts shifted to her biological mother. I was personally acquainted with her loss and the pain that must be in her heart.

As we got closer, I became so nervous. "Are you ready to see our little girl?" Rick asked.

He was way too calm.

The foster mother welcomed us into her home and said, "She's napping right now, but if you'd like, you may peek in." We stood over her crib and looked down at her curly blond hair. Rick reached over the crib ever so gently and brushed her locks away from her eyes. We examined her delicate, pudgy fingers and counted them. I felt as if we gave birth that day.

She opened her eyes and looked up, now examining us. I reached over the crib to pick her up, and she held out her tiny arms. The miracle of bonding began. Still sleepy, she rested her head on my shoulder. Rick pulled us both closer to him, and we snuggled.

Katie Rose Mae was entrusted to us 13 years after we had given our own biological daughter to her adoptive parents.

Rick picked up the phone that was left dangling that May morning. There was a tone of protective anger as he asked, "Who is this?" The social worker patiently introduced herself again and explained, "The child you gave up for adoption 22 years ago desires to contact you."

He shouted, "Why, that's great news!" I looked up from the floor and caught a tear in his eye. I said to him, "Honey, we need more time!" I felt so unprepared and scared—just like the day she was born. A multitude of conflicting emotions surfaced.

Rick helped me off the floor, and as he lifted my arms and put them around his big shoulders, he said, "This is the day the Lord has made just for us, Gloria." He was right.

We wondered how her adoptive parents felt. A card arrived from them a few weeks later. Jim and Dorothy had named her Angelina. They ended their note by saying, "We want to thank you from the bottom of our hearts for the gift you gave us, and we have loved her very much."

I went to the post office to pick up our first letter from Angelina. As my fingers ran over her handwriting, I began to sob. I'm not sure why, but I even smelled the letter. Was this really happening? I opened it slowly, and a picture fell out. The last time I looked at her she was a precious newborn. Now before my eyes, she was a woman.

It was important to her that we meet on her birthday. As she stepped out of the car, I walked toward her. In spite of her courage to meet us, I sensed her fear.

"It's been a long time," she said softly.

"Yes, honey, it has. Are you okay with this?"

"It's as if I just found a puzzle piece that I have been looking for," she answered.

I reached out to her and we carefully embraced, both of us shivering from the intense joy we felt. I could have sworn I saw the same tears on her that we left so many years ago. Rick wrapped his arms around both of us, and we cried.

It was a miracle and nothing less. Rick and I believe it was a result of our steadfast prayers and the courage of two women. For an unwed mother to choose life for her baby and give the gift of a child to another is, and will always be, the epitome of courage.

Rick and I, against all the odds, are still side by side 35 years after our first baby was born. We see so clearly now God's sustaining hand of mercy in our years of waiting and wondering. He brought us full circle by allowing us to know the pain of losing, the joy of receiving, and the miracle of reuniting.

Some moms realize early on, in praying for a child, to seek this special gift through the world of adoption. As with birth, the event is sometimes a long and painful one. For the Davises, it was unusually rocky. But they never faltered in their belief that God would provide them a child to love.

↭ *A Child to Love* ↝

BY CHARLENE DAVIS, GOLDENROD, FLORIDA

After several years of dealing with issues of infertility, my husband and I embarked on a life-altering journey through the trials and tribulations of adoption. Although the process was stressful and painful, we found beauty in it. Our love for each other and the love of our families and friends grew in abundance. Our faith in God was strengthened and increased. In addition, we met many wonderful people to help guide us through the process—people who ordinarily would not have crossed our path.

In the beginning, we had several "nibbles" that got us excited and helped to keep our spirits up. Friends at our church had a niece who was considering placing her baby for adoption, but she and her family decided to keep the baby. At one point, we almost had an opportunity to adopt 11-month-old triplets! The birth mother was very young, single, and overwhelmed with the responsibility of caring for triplets. She had decided to give them up for adoption. When we accepted, however, she had a change of heart and kept her babies.

Right around the Christmas holidays, a young, single girl selected us to adopt her baby. This time the birth father kept changing his mind about giving his consent. Just after Christmas, we received a call saying the birth mother had gone into labor and that she still wanted to go through with the placement. We were also informed the birth father was now being cooperative.

Our day was spent celebrating. We had fun shopping for last-minute items for the nursery, telling perfect strangers in restaurants and stores that we were in labor. Late that night, we received a call saying we had a healthy baby girl. We were delirious with joy, thanksgiving, and happiness. Phone calls were made to family members. Everyone was crying and rejoicing that our dream of having a family had finally come true. We waited impatiently for someone to call and tell us to come and get our baby girl.

The call never came. With no means of supporting the baby, the birth father convinced the birth mother to keep the child. The birth mother took home a baby she had not planned on keeping and went to live with her mother. We still pray for that little girl. She will always carry a piece of our hearts around with her. We also pray for her brave young mother.

Five months later, we hopped back on the roller coaster again. Our attorney called and said another birth mother had chosen us to adopt her baby. Shortly after, the birth mother went to a different adoption agency and picked a couple who offered her a financial settlement. We don't know if the other couple ever knew the birth mother was working with us, or if they knew this woman was trying to play "Let's Make a Deal." When the birth mother called our attorney and asked if we would like to make a counteroffer, he strongly advised us to withdraw from this dangerous situation. It made us very sad to think this birth mother put a price on her baby's head. Although we grieved again over the loss of another child, we were consoled by knowing that the baby was placed in a good, loving home with people like us who very much wanted a child to love.

A few weeks later, our attorney called again and said a young woman had just delivered a baby boy and wanted to place him for adoption. There were problems during the delivery and the little fellow was sick, so there was a possibility of a lengthy hospital stay. It took us all of two seconds to think about it. Of course we wanted to adopt him. Later that night, our attorney called and told us that our little guy was doing much, much better. He was still in intensive care, but they expected a good, if not complete recovery. Praise the Lord! What wonderful news.

The next morning, we anxiously waited by the phone for the call, announcing that the birth mother had signed the consent forms to place this sweet child in our hearts and home. However, the call we received told us the birth mother had a change of heart during the night and decided to keep her baby. We were crushed. While we certainly couldn't fault this woman for wanting to keep her little boy, we were left wondering how many pieces of our hearts were left to break.

We didn't understand why we or other couples had to go through this kind of turmoil. With each incident, however, our faith and our marriage grew stronger. We were grieving, but we were also blessed by love and support from our families and friends. As children of God, we knew then, as we know today, that we can stand on His promise: "Delight yourself in the LORD and he will give you the desires of your heart" (Psalm 37:4).

While we were grieving over our latest loss, the Lord was speaking to the birth mother's heart. Ultimately she decided we could give her son the kind of home she could not provide. Hallelujah! This courageous young woman is lifted up every day in our prayers, as well as in our son's prayers. He is now a bright, energetic, and very talkative eight-year-old boy who knows how much his birth mother loved him...so much that she let him go. What a beautiful testimony to a mother's unconditional love. A day doesn't pass without us lifting up birth mothers around the world in prayer. They have not only chosen to give life to their children, but they have also chosen to give their children a life.

Countless lives were touched by our journey and by seeing God's plan as it unfolded. We received hundreds of cards and gifts from all over the country, even from people we did not know. He truly is our miracle baby, and he is proof positive that the Lord hears us and answers our prayers—all in good time, all in God's time. Even when we didn't understand the events taking place, we remained faithful to Him. We believed "Thy will be done," and He rewarded us with the most cherished gift of all: a child to love.

Our children will always be our children, no matter how old they are. When our children begin having children of their own, we must step back and allow them to make their own decisions. How difficult that can be at times, but Karen learned through prayer that her daughter was also God's child, and He would see to her safety. Karen also learned that many times God answers prayer in very unexpected ways.

Hezekiah and I

BY KAREN STRAND, LACEY, WASHINGTON

I remember the birth of my daughter's first baby, delivered by cesarean section. One year later, when she got the news she was pregnant with her second child, Julie was adamant about giving birth "the normal way."

"I want to experience natural childbirth, Mom. I don't even want to consider another cesarean." My daughter explained a new procedure called VBAC, vaginal birth after cesarean, and told me it was perfectly safe, offering birth mothers another option.

"I'm just not comfortable with this, Julie," I told her. "The last I heard it was 'once cesarean, always cesarean.'"

"You're so old-fashioned." Julie brushed off my concerns. "Doctors are doing this all the time now."

I decided to do some research of my own and looked up the statistics regarding the VBAC procedure. The information only served to confirm my worries about the possible risk of a uterine rupture.

"I'm really concerned, Julie. I don't feel right about this." I didn't want to tell my daughter what to do, but I did want to present the possible dangers of her decision. "What does your doctor think you should do?"

"He thinks I should have another cesarean."

Nothing could sway Julie's decision—not my old-fashioned concerns, Internet statistics, or her doctor's advice. Determined to go ahead with her plans, she switched to another doctor who was willing to accommodate her desire for natural childbirth.

My concerns continued to escalate, and I prayed for Julie's safety daily. "Oh Lord, protect my daughter and her unborn child."

One morning while I was making the bed, I was mulling over some Bible verses from a recent devotional. In the Old Testament, King Hezekiah knew God was with him, yet when he received a threatening letter from the king of Assyria, he didn't just ask vaguely for protection. Instead "he went up to the temple of the LORD and spread it out before the LORD" (2 Kings 19:14).

That's what I need to do. Sinking down on the edge of the bed, I bowed my head and "laid my letter before God." In true Hezekiah fashion, I prayed, "'Give ear, O LORD, and hear; open your eyes, O LORD, and see' (2 Kings 19:16). You know every detail of this situation that has troubled me from the start. My daughter wants to have this VBAC, but it doesn't sound safe to me. Her previous doctor even advised against it. But there's no one who can change her mind—no one except You, Lord. I give You this entire matter. So if I am wrong, and having the baby naturally is best, then I step aside. But if this is not best for her or the baby, then, O Lord, I pray You will intervene and allow only the best for them both."

Finally I was at peace.

Julie's due date arrived with no signs of imminent labor. Ten days later she was doing everything she could think of to promote labor, and still no contractions.

Her current doctor continued to monitor Julie closely, and finally advised her to have her second cesarean section. Reluctantly she scheduled one.

One day before her check-in date, my daughter changed her mind. "Maybe if I wait just a few more days, I still might go into labor." She was very discouraged, but even the additional few days didn't change things, and Julie headed to the hospital with her husband, Jeff.

I was privileged to accompany Julie and my son-in-law into the operating room to celebrate my grandchild's birth. What I heard from behind the drape shot through the room like a bullet.

"Julie," the doctor said, "your old surgical scar is completely separated. Your womb is extremely thin. If we had attempted a VBAC, the baby would not have survived, and neither would you."

The nurse explained that Julie's uterus would have ruptured, and the hemorrhaging would have been so great that both my daughter and the baby would have died within minutes.

Tears rolled down Julie's cheeks, and I marveled over everything that she had done to prevent the cesarean section. But despite my daughter's decision, God knew her desire to have a healthy baby. I am so grateful He heard my prayers and kept the baby inside until the right way, the best way, was accomplished.

I welcomed my newborn granddaughter, Janna Michelle Schultz, with tears of joy in my eyes and a thankful heart.

Lynette knew the Lord would answer her prayer for a child. If she was losing this baby, she knew He would provide another child one day. She knew He was hearing her cries. The Lord showed her just how much He listened.

⌒ *The Artful Dodger* ⌒

BY LYNETTE MARIE GALISEWSKI, LITTLETON, COLORADO

"Lord, You know how much I want a baby, yet here I am on an operating table being prepped for surgery to remove the lifeless embryo inside me." The pain was deep.

Ed and I were so ecstatic to discover that we were pregnant, and we were already trying names on our growing baby. We imagined games of peekaboo and hide-and-seek, and cozy family snuggles on the couch. Barely had these sugarplum visions danced in our heads, before the music came to a dead halt. Our baby was proclaimed a "blighted ovum," like a construction project that had run out of building materials. Simply put, I had suffered a miscarriage.

We didn't want to believe it, so we sought ultrasounds and experts to read the results. All of them agreed: no viable embryo. Given my age (late thirties) and our desire to start a family, we opted for a procedure called dilatation and curettage, or D and C. This would expedite the recovery process so we could try to have another baby quickly. Our Christian obstetrician scheduled the procedure at St. Joseph's Hospital in Orange, California, not far from where we lived. Disappointed but reconciled to our situation, Ed and I drove to the appointment, both of us feeling deplete of emotion. We clasped hands and prayed, surrendering the outcome to God, asking for a future pregnancy that would result in a healthy baby.

Lying on the table alone, I continued praying, "Lord, there's always risk with an operation like this. Please protect my body from harm. Guide the surgeon's hands according to Your perfect will." Those were my last whispers of desire as the anesthesia melted my mind into that timeless place of oblivion. Waking up in what seemed to me seconds later, I felt Ed's hand caressing my forehead.

"What a trouper you are, Lynette! You snored your way through the whole operation."

I attempted a grin, but between the medication and the feelings of loss that no surgical knife could remove, I could only acknowledge his words with my eyes. The lab reports strangely showed "no products of conception." As I had had bleeding, we wrote that off to having already miscarried before the surgery.

Three weeks passed with continual follow-up appointments. The procedure left me with some residual bleeding, so my doctor continued to check my blood levels. After my last test, I received a frenzied call from the doctor to meet her at the hospital as soon as possible. The HCG levels in my blood were rising, an indication of a continued pregnancy, possibly in a fallopian tube. Ed and I raced to the hospital, and once again I was prepped for surgery.

They wheeled me into the ultrasound center to determine exactly where the tubal pregnancy was located. Unaware of my situation, the technician cheerfully pointed to a mass in my uterus and proclaimed, "Here's your little bundle of joy. Looks like a boy—he's quite the swimmer. Look at him move! I would say you're about ten weeks along now."

My husband and I looked at each other, not knowing whether to celebrate for joy or cry out in fear. So many questions rushed through our minds. Where was this baby when the ultrasounds pronounced him nonexistent? How did he survive the cutting, scraping, and suction of the D and C? Was he healthy and whole? Would the traumatized placenta be able to nourish him to full term?

"God is in control, Lynette." My husband comforted me with his words. "And we're going to trust Him with our little guy."

I remembered my prayer on the operating table. "Guide the doctor's hands," I had prayed, and He did. Our little one apparently was quite the swimmer—alive and well just ten weeks into gestation. Our baby artfully dodged the surgery that for all intents and purposes should have scraped everything from my uterus.

We decided to celebrate this pregnancy, much to our doctor's delight and the hospital's relief, praying daily for a healthy baby.

Braun Adam Galisewski made it to 36 weeks inside my highly compromised womb, and weighed three pounds, thirteen ounces at birth. He was more scrawn than brawn, but amazingly unscathed. He did not have a single scar from his intrauterine battle for survival.

Today Braun is a strapping young man, 15 years old, with a fascination for clashing swords and military maneuvers. On the hockey rink, Braun is known as the "Artful Dodger." And, many thanks to the Lord, we know just how true that is.

Praying for a child has to be the most abundant prayer God hears from a woman. How many He hears on any given day can only be imagined. He will answer those requests in His own time and exactly how He wants to. Peggie learned that just when she thought it was too late.

∽ *A Blue-Ribbon Bundle for Mom* ∾

BY PEGGIE C. BOHANON, SPRINGFIELD, MISSOURI

God has always kept His promises to me, with many a surprising twist or turn along the way: an unexpected vacation to change my life, a career to exceed my plans, a loving husband to fulfill my dreams. Peace in fear, hope in despair, light in darkness—these are the surprises of love you receive when Christ is your Savior and Lord.

Sometimes God's surprises come in little packages as red-faced, screaming bundles of joy. And that is where my story begins.

At 41 years of age, I welcomed Joey, our firstborn child. He was a wonderful, healthy child and perfect—well, almost! We quickly learned the necessary parenting skills: how to late-night feed, diaper a bottom, assemble a toy, and find all the great baby garage-sale items!

But the dream was not complete. We wanted two children, a boy and a girl. So with anticipation and prayer we watched and waited for a little girl to complete our family.

Age 41 quickly passed to 42, and I began to panic. Were we crazy at our age to want another child? No, God had placed this dream in our hearts, and we would hold on to it.

One Sunday night at church, in desperation I lifted my hands to God and prayed, "Lord, please give us a healthy baby girl." In my heart I heard the words, "It's done; it's done; it's done."

I shared this amazing promise with my husband. We both cried and rejoiced. Perhaps I was pregnant even now.

In due time I discovered I wasn't! Month after month rolled by as I became more and more discouraged. I cried, prayed, and questioned. My dear husband became my "solid rock." He would say, "God told you it would happen, and He will keep His promise. But He will do it in His time."

But time is running out, I thought. *I am 43. Does God remember that?*

Still nothing happened. Then one weekend I felt ill with what I thought was the flu. My dad, a retired pastor, earnestly prayed for God's deliverance. I soon discovered that in nine months I would be delivered of...you guessed it: a blessed little bundle!

After almost two years since God's promise, our joy knew no bounds. Everyone carefully monitored the progress of this 43-year-old pregnant woman. Each morning our family gathered to pray, "And God bless little Aimee and help her to grow."

How I anticipated the coming event! As the baby started growing, I started shopping for tiny red hair bows and a darling red-velvet dress (on sale, so how could I resist?).

On October 21, 1984, on our wedding anniversary, it became apparent Baby Bohanon was about to join our family. We sped to the hospital, and after three and a half hours, I heard the doctor say, "Congratulations! You have a beautiful baby boy!"

Boy? I was relieved, happy...and stunned! Thank You, God, for giving us a healthy baby boy. But Lord, what about the little girl I thought You were sending? I shared my struggles, questions, and tears with my husband. Then we prayed, thanking God for Jason, our new baby boy, gladly accepting His will.

Unanswered questions remained, but were soon replaced with a faithful Father's peace and joy. In God's eternal plan and sovereignty, this child was to be Jason, not Aimee. He had been in God's heart and mind long before my plea, the conception, and Jason's birth. I could trust Him to keep His promises and to know what was best.

I began to smile, and I have been smiling ever since. Jason is 20 now, a 6-foot, 6-inch college junior, full of fun and great mischief, and most of all, he loves the Lord. I would not trade my bright-eyed Jason for all the red-hair-bowed Aimees in the world. And he sure would have hated that red-velvet dress!

God answered the prayer of this mom the day He sent me a surprise package, wrapped up in love and tied in blue!

3
Life Lessons

MOMS ARE THE ORIGINAL TEACHERS and cheerleaders. When our children succeed, so do we. When our children suffer, we would take their pain in a heartbeat. Wouldn't it be nice if when we turn our hearts over to God, life became a bed of roses with no more worries, no more troubles, no more painful lessons to be learned? But some of the best lessons, the most incredible miracles and true successes for our children, come after hours, days, months, and sometimes even years on our knees before the Lord. He knows and loves our children even more than we do (as hard as that is to fathom), and He planned for them long before the foundation of the world. We may be totally surprised at how and where He works His wonders in our children's lives, but we should never be surprised at the amazing things He will do when we put our children in His hands. When we pray to *hear* God's voice through the tough times, one of the lessons we will learn is to *recognize* His voice. And what better teacher could there be?

Beloved, do not be surprised at the fiery ordeal among you, which comes upon you for your testing, as though some strange thing

*were happening to you; but to the degree that you share the suffer-
ings of Christ, keep on rejoicing, so that also at the revelation of
His glory you may rejoice with exultation.*

1 PETER 4:12-13 NASB

A mom's children are her most prized possessions. She will pray for the very best things in life to happen to them. When these best things happen, they may come in an unexpected package!

∽ What I Didn't Pray For ∽

BY PEGGYSUE WELLS, ROANOKE, INDIANA

Nelma's fifth baby, a little boy, was whisked away from the delivery room as soon as it was born. "Where is my son? I want to see my son," she told the doctor.

The doctor told her that perhaps it was best that she not see him. He was born deformed and, with the complications involved, they should consider putting the child in an institution to be cared for. "I want to see my son," she insisted.

So the new bundle was brought and placed in Nelma's arms. She smelled the sweet new baby smell of him, cooing to the little boy and cradling him to her heart. Then ever so carefully, she unwrapped his blanket. There lay her infant son, born without legs and with arms not fully developed. Nelma took it all in, caressed his soft, new skin, and smiled into his trusting eyes.

"Oh," she smiled softly, "is that all?"

So newborn Jerry went home with his parents, where he was welcomed into the loving arms of his family. There were struggles along the way, just as there are with all families. Some were harder to deal with than others, but through them all Jerry grew and flourished with the help of his family and friends and many, many prayers.

Before anyone realized it, Jerry was ready to go off to college. One day at church Nelma was talking with her friend Barbara and discovered that Barbara's daughter, Kathi, went to the same college. Barbara told Jerry to make sure he connected with Kathi at school, and she would help him learn his way around the campus. This started a friendship that would last a long, long time.

A year later while home on a visit, Kathi broke down in tears while talking with her mom.

"Mom, Jerry wants to marry me. I know he loves me and I love him. But Mom, Jerry doesn't have any legs. Can you marry someone without legs?"

Barbara smiled as she looked at her lovely, grown daughter.

"Honey, ever since you were little, I have prayed for you, for your present, and for your future. I have prayed for just the right man to be your husband. I prayed he would be strong in character and integrity. I prayed he would be a leader in his home and community. I prayed he would provide well for you and your children. I prayed your future husband would know God and he would be an honest and hard worker. I prayed he would love you and be a tender life's partner. Most of all, I prayed he would be your best friend as well as your husband." Barbara paused to lift Kathi's chin so their eyes met. "But, Kathi dearest, I never prayed he would have legs."

With the blessing and prayers of their parents, Jerry and Kathi were married. Today they live in California. Jerry is an elder in their church and works as a teacher. They have five beautiful children and a wonderful marriage.

A lot of the credit for the success of their family came from their mothers: Nelma, who saw not her son's handicaps but his potential, and Barbara, who saw not the wheelchair but the man it held.

In the blink of an eye, we send a prayer up to the Lord. "Hurry, Lord, help me now!" How He answers is always a joy to discover, especially when it comes to answering the inquisitive questions of a child.

～ Eight Years' Worth of Love ～

BY CAROL DAVIS GUSTKE, BATTLE CREEK, MICHIGAN

The troubled eyes of my eight-year-old son stared up at me as I tucked him in bed for the night. It was at these times we shared the day's events and ended with a quiet prayer.

"Why the serious face, Luke? Did something special happen today?"

He nervously bit the corner of his lip and snuggled further down into his covers.

"Mom," he began hesitantly, "is it okay if I don't love Jesus a lot?"

His question startled me, and for a moment I didn't answer. I sensed he needed more than a mother's pat on the head or a kiss on the cheek to cure his uneasiness.

Settling myself on the edge of his bed, I silently said a prayer: *Lord, please give me the wisdom I need to answer his question.* God's answer was immediate, almost taking my breath away.

"Luke," I began slowly, "when you were born, did you know your daddy and me?"

"No," he murmured softly, shaking his head.

"Do you remember us taking care of you?"

Again he shook his head. I gently squeezed his hand and smiled.

"Of course you don't, and that's the way it's supposed to be. But your daddy and I knew you and loved you very much. When you were hungry, we fed you. When it was cold outside, we wrapped you in warm blankets. When you had a tummy ache, we rocked you to sleep. We didn't ask you to love us back. We just loved you.

"But do you know what began to happen?"

Luke had been listening closely from the beginning. Now his curiosity was stirred even more. "Tell me," he urged.

"Well, as you grew older, you learned to recognize us. You would hold out your arms when we walked into your room. Your very first words were *Mama* and *Dada*. It wasn't long before you were giving love back to us, even though it was just a baby's worth of love. The longer you knew us, the more you loved us."

The familiar hush I often felt when the Lord was teaching me something washed over my soul. "That's how it is in loving Jesus. When you are born into His family, you know very little about Him. He loves you and takes care of you like a newborn baby. As you pray to Him and read His Word, you begin to know Him and love Him back. The longer you know Him, the more you love Him."

Luke cocked his head to one side and gave me a long, thoughtful look.

"Then it's okay if I only love Him eight years' worth?" he asked.

"That's just perfect, son," I answered, quickly blinking back the tears. Luke heaved a heavy sigh of relief.

"Mom, you sure know how to answer my questions good!"

I left Luke's room in awe of God's wonderful wisdom. Someday when he was old enough, I would explain this day to him—how he had asked a little boy's question, and the Lord had answered my prayer in the blink of an eye, giving me the perfect "grown-up" answer!

Those of us who are moms have all prayed at one time or another for faithful and kindhearted friends for our children. What we usually do not ask for is how we want their friends to look. But Debbie did, and she was surprised when God chose to ignore her requests.

⌁ Answered Prayer in an Unexpected Package ⌁

BY DEBBIE HANNAH SKINNER, AMARILLO, TEXAS

The phone call that evening sent shock waves through my soul. Amidst the weeping on the other end of the line, I could hardly understand the almost inaudible voice.

"My dad!...My dad!...He's...he's...dead!" cried a hysterical, grieving girl.

It took me a few moments to finally realize who was calling. Then I recognized the voice. It was Susan, my daughter's best friend who lived in another state.

Just moments before the phone call, Susan learned her father had passed away in a tragic accident. The teenager was devastated, and my heart ached for her.

My daughter got on the phone in the kitchen, and we both spoke and cried with Susan for some time, trying to provide love and comfort for her as best we could. As the conversation ended, we assured her we loved her and would be praying for her.

Susan had spent a lot of time in our home before reluctantly moving to Southern California with her mother after her parents' divorce the year before. I had grown to know and love this precious teenager and was deeply touched because, even though we hadn't seen her in months, our home was one of the first places she called outside her own family to share the tragic news.

I was struck with a sense of deep sadness for Susan, a teenager now without a dad. In the emotional mix was also a debt of gratitude to God for bringing Susan into our lives. But there was another feeling welling up in me as well: embarrassment. You see, Susan was an answer to prayer that was so unexpected that I almost missed her when she came.

Several years earlier we were new to town, and I watched in heart-wrenching agony as my daughter tried to establish new friendships. It seemed everyone already had friends from childhood, and she was the outsider, the new kid on the block, the odd man out. It was a difficult time for her, as every attempt at making new friends was rejected.

That's when I began to pray for God to send a special friend her way.

I didn't want just *anyone* to be her new friend, mind you. I wanted a companion for my daughter like the special friends I had had when I was growing up—a friend like Rosemary, whom I laughed with on countless sleepovers, or one like Madelene, whom I could talk with on just about any subject under the sun, or perhaps someone similar to my girlfriend Melville, who was such a great listener and had a kind and gentle spirit.

Unfortunately my prayer for my daughter's friend came with strings attached, even though I didn't realize it at the time. Those strings were my expectations for what this friend would be like: family untouched by divorce, active in church, *blah, blah, blah*. Basically, I wanted a friend for my child whose family life was a carbon copy of my own. The list of spoken and unspoken qualifications went on and on.

Isn't it strange how we can pray and impose restrictions on the God of the universe as to exactly when and how and where He should answer our prayers? That's what I did.

There's nothing wrong with praying boldly and specifically, but I've found that when I pray with a choke hold on my expectations, I can miss the answer to my prayer when God chooses to deliver His response in an unexpected, unanticipated way. Susan taught me this. When she showed up on the scene, she wasn't packaged in the exact way I expected her to come. That's how I almost missed her.

It took quite a while for me to realize it, but even though Susan could not initially check off every item on my invisible "Application for Friendship with My Daughter" form, she was an absolutely perfect fit as a friend for my girl.

Susan once accompanied us on a family vacation to the mountains and was an absolute joy to be around the entire week. She modeled good manners and concern for other people during the whole trip. On another occasion, even though it was unfamiliar territory, she enthusiastically went to church camp with my child and had a blast. She felt God tugging on her heart one night around a campfire and responded by placing her faith in Christ. My daughter is quite a talker and Susan is a fabulous listener (something I hadn't even noted on my expectations list). I could gush on and on about Susan's fine character qualities, but the bottom line is that she is a wonderful young woman and a "perfect-fit friend" for my child, beyond my wildest expectations.

As I have watched their friendship grow over time, I've become increasingly grateful for God's answer to prayer wrapped in the package of Susan. I would smile to myself when I'd hear the laughter drifting from my daughter's room late into the night during their sleepovers. When Susan shared the news that she was moving to California, I don't know who was the most upset…my daughter or me.

The incident with Susan reminds me that God most certainly knows what my child needs more than I do. That's what Jesus was talking about in Matthew 7:9-11 when He said, "Which of you, if his son asks for bread, will give him a stone? Or if he asks for a fish, will give him a snake? If you, then, though you are evil, know how to give good gifts to your children, how much more will your Father in heaven give good gifts to those who ask him!"

Susan was back in town visiting recently and stopped by our home. She has grown into a beautiful young woman, inside and out. Seeing her again reminded me of how God had not only provided a good gift for my child through the gift of friendship, but also had provided a lesson for me on prayer. It was a lesson about the importance of asking God to provide for my child, then *trusting Him* to do so in the way He saw was best, even when it didn't meet my narrow expectations.

The Lord sees what I cannot. He knows what I do not. He can be trusted to give good gifts to my child. I just need to pray, trust Him, and then be on the lookout for how He creatively chooses to package His answer.

We pray and pray for a child of our own, to hold and raise and love. When God does not answer our prayer just as we want, we sometimes lose our bearings. With the help of a friend, Judy saw just how well the Lord had answered her prayers!

∽ *A Spiritual Mom* ∾

BY JUDY GANN, LAKEWOOD, WASHINGTON

Mother's Day dawned bright and beautiful for everyone but me. I drove into the church parking lot, turned off the ignition, and sat immobile, my hands gripping the steering wheel. *Lord, I can't do this.* For seven years I had avoided this moment.

I had always wanted to be a mother. As a young girl happily playing house with my baby sister and my dolls, I dreamed of the day when I would have my own children. After becoming a Christian, the recurring prayer of my heart became, *Father, please bring me a godly husband and children. I long to be a mom.*

Yet I remained single. A children's librarian, I focused my mothering capacities on the children who populated my world every day. I treasured time spent with my niece and nephew.

For many years I also experienced the blessing of mentoring several young women from my church. One-on-one and in small groups, these girls shared their hearts with me—their joys, sorrows, and spiritual struggles.

Surrounded by children in the library and the girls I mentored, I shoved the issue of having children on the back shelf of my mind until, in my early 40s, I had a necessary hysterectomy.

I was blindsided by the cavernous void in my life following surgery. The finality of the hysterectomy and the emptiness of my childless state seared my mind. *God, what happened to my prayer? Why didn't You answer it?*

Aching with inner pain, I struggled as the sight of babies in the grocery store, at church, and even in the library ignited my sense of loss. Waves of grief, anger, and despair assaulted me. I plummeted into a deep depression.

In time and with the help of a compassionate counselor, I realized that my sense of worth and value to God and other people is not based on motherhood, but rather on my relationship with the Lord. The God who created me loves me—married or single, a mother or childless. In God's eyes, I am not less of a woman because I'm not a mother. I began to concentrate on the gifts God has given me, instead of focusing on what might be "missing" in my life.

But one last remnant of pain remained. I refused to attend church on Mother's Day. As each Mother's Day approached, I argued with God. *Lord, it hurts too much. I dread sitting alone when the mothers stand and are celebrated. What if I break down and cry?* It was easier to stay away. Soon staying home on Mother's Day became an entrenched habit.

Then at a women's retreat, I listened intently as Jeanne, the speaker, spoke about attending the first Mother's Day church service after her mother's death. Single at the time, she told of the unexpected comfort she had found at church that morning and, yes, even the tears she needed to shed. I thought to myself, *If Jeanne can do it, maybe I can do it.*

Now, after seven years, I had finally made it as far as the church parking lot. Conflicting emotions battled within me as my reluctant legs carried me across the parking lot and into the church foyer. Once inside, I froze at the sight of children handing a flower to each mother. I stepped back, ready to bolt out the door.

Austin, a boy from my preschool story-time group, shyly approached with a carnation. "No thank you, Austin," I whispered. "I'm not a mother."

My eyes flooded with tears. Yet with an inner strength and calm from God alone, I turned to walk up the stairs to the sanctuary.

Suddenly I felt an arm across my shoulders. I turned and gazed with blurry eyes into the face of Barbara, the mother of one of the young women I had mentored.

"Judy," she said, in a soft, but firm voice, "you *are* a mother. You're Carla's *spiritual mother*." Barbara waved to Austin, who returned with his fistful of flowers. My hand shook as I took the flower Austin held out to me.

This time tears of joy welled up as I climbed the steps to the sanctuary, proudly clutching my yellow carnation. *Spiritual mother.* As I slid into a pew, the names of the young women I mentored paraded through my mind: Masako, Carla, Jennifer, Sarah, and Lori. What a joy to come alongside these young women, nurturing them by example and sharing from my walk with the Lord.

God didn't answer my prayer for children, at least not as I had hoped or imagined. But in the quiet moments before the start of the church service, I realized He had answered this deepest prayer of my heart in a special and unique way. God showed me that the word *mother* could be defined in many ways. I will never give birth to a child. But as a *spiritual mother*, I have the rich privilege of nurturing and influencing the children and young people God places in my life. A meal with my niece and nephew or an afternoon with one of the young women in my Bible study offers precious opportunities for spiritual mothering.

Joy replaced grief as I settled in for my first Mother's Day church service in many years. *Lord, thank You for the privilege of being a spiritual mom.*

*This story was published in *Woman's Touch*, May/June 2004.

We watch our children grow under our careful guidance. We encourage them, teach them, and most of all pray for them. Pam and Bill prayed that they were doing the best they could. The Lord showed them just how right they were.

⌇ *The Making of an MVP* ⌇

BY PAM FARREL, SAN MARCOS, CALIFORNIA

I believe God hears the desperate prayers of a mother's heart. When Bill and I married, both from non-Christian homes, then I became pregnant, we prayed, "God, parent us so we can parent our children. You know the brokenness we come from. We want it to stop with us in this generation. Show us how to build character into our children." We asked, "God, what traits, what character qualities, what practical skills do our children need to have in their lives by the time they are 18 so they can soar with You?"

Then Bill and I brainstormed a long list of traits. Next I took that list and I wrote a graduation prayer to read to Brock when he turned 18 or at his high-school graduation. Here is an excerpt:

A Graduation Prayer

I pray that you will have embraced and lived out your own faith in Jesus....I want you to have fallen in love with your Savior firsthand, not relying on Mom and Dad's faith but a strong faith of your own. I want you to know the joy of walking moment by moment in the power of the Holy Spirit. I pray for you to be able to discern God's will for yourself, to have a rich prayer life. I pray for you to really believe prayer works. By the time you are 18, I pray you have influenced others and have seen how a prayer movement can begin with just one— YOU! I want you to have had and now enjoy great friendships—the kind of friends that will die for you or you for them. I pray for you to have the courage and confidence to be a leader among your friends so they might draw nearer to Jesus because of you, and to love God's Word and have so much confidence with the Word that you have taught it to others. I pray for you to know the joy of sharing your faith. I want you to know the thrill of walking in obedience to God. To find the gifts He's given you, to discern His will, to carve out your own ministry. I desire to see you put others first...and if it is necessary to, I pray you'll have the courage of a Daniel, or a Joseph, and stand alone for your faith. I pray you will, above all else, keep a good name and good reputation. I pray you will understand the huge price that was paid by this country's forefathers and be an involved citizen. Be a leader as I have prepared you, with all God's compassion and wisdom for this day.

Bill and I decided to make character-building a fun, positive family activity, so we created Learner and Leader Day. It's one day a year where we have a fun family activity, negotiating privileges and responsibilities for the year. We choose one character quality on the list we created, and we focus on helping a specific child internalize that quality for the coming year. Having just one main quality makes it easier to remember, and it also seems possible for the child. It can become too easy to raise the bar higher and higher on a child, so that what started out to be a good thing turns into unrealistic expectations (followed by rebellion).

So we choose one trait: honesty, integrity, initiative, sharing their faith, etc. After we have chosen the quality (and from their freshman year on they have input into the quality they think they need to work on), we then choose a verse for the year. (Again, from ten years old on, we teach them how to choose their own verse.) That is the verse we pray over them for the following year. It's posted many places: on their lunch box or in their locker, on the refrigerator, on my mirror or their bedroom door—wherever I think will help us all remember to pray!

The final, but I believe the most important component from the children's point of view, is we give a gift that encourages and empowers them to live out the unique calling we see God layering into their life. Bill and I truly believe that by the time a child is 13, he or she should have a platform that is something the child feels great about, that can be used to help the child share Jesus.

We saw that one of the common factors in the kids that did well in our high-school youth group is that they had parents that prayed and lived lives of integrity, and they had parents who encouraged them to be on the "offense" not "defense," meaning, the parents initiated ways for the students to bring God into their students' life and world in a fun way.

Some families hosted pool parties for the youth group, others ran backpack trips, and some jumped in and helped with youth leadership groups. Other moms just made some really great food after each Friday-night game. But all played an active part.

So on Learner and Leader Day, year after year, as Bill and I prayed for Brock, we kept seeing athletics as his bent. The verses we prayed for him were things like "Run in such a way as you might win," or "Excel still more," and we gave him gifts to train and resource him like a gym bag or *Sports Spectrum* magazine (a Christian sports magazine).

Then we layered prayer into our lives and the lives of our children at every level. We always said grace at meals, we prayed each night with them at bedtime, we prayed over them as they left for school, we prayed before big events in their lives.

Here is a snapshot of how God has answered those prayers: I was at the first football game in which Brock was to be the starting varsity quarterback. Brock had heard reports that the Supreme Court had restricted football players from saying a prayer before a game in Texas. Brock thought that was a wrong decision. He especially thought it was wrong in light of the school shootings across the nation the prior spring.

Brock decided he wanted to take a stand. He called up his buddies on the team and said, "After the game, I am going to the 50-yard line to pray. Will you join me? I am calling all the guys on the other team, too. So win or lose, can I count on you to be at the 50?" They all said, "You bet. We're there for ya, man!"

Brock's team lost 38-0. After the game, the team was discouraged, disappointed, and disillusioned. The coach tried to round them up, but Brock went straight to the 50-yard line and knelt down, all alone.

My heart ached at the sight of my son kneeling alone at the 50. Out loud I said to Bill, "Honey, he's all alone!"

Tears streamed down my cheeks, a mixture of empathy and pride. Then I remembered the prayer we had prayed years ago before Brock was born: "Help him stand alone for You, God."

After a moment's hesitation, three players from the opposing team joined Brock at the 50 and they prayed. They prayed!

I ran down to my son and threw my arms around Brock's tall, sweaty body. Reaching up, I took his face in my hands and said, "I have never been more proud of you than I am at this moment. I know tonight was one of the hardest nights of your life. I know you are disappointed at the loss, and that your team was distracted by it, so they did not join you at the 50. But you kept your word to God."

The next week I had a speaking engagement and was out of town, so I asked Bill to have Brock call me from the field after the game. At 2:00 AM I got a call on my cell phone. "Mom, we won! And there were about *40* of us praying at the 50 tonight!"

Brock and his teammates continued to pray at the 50, and a few weeks later on a Wednesday, our phone rang at 6:00 AM. "Have you seen the paper?" our friend exclaimed. Brock had been named as *Athlete of the Week* in San Diego's newspaper.

Later that day my house was filled with freshman football players. Zach had given his personal testimony, and now Brock was sharing his. Brock held up some newspaper shots of him passing the ball, but the last one he held up was the *Athlete of the Week* clipping. Then he said, as he passed it around the room, "Guys, there's one thing for sure. I do not know how, I do not know when, but remember, those who honor God, God honors."

At Brock's high-school graduation, we asked him why he thought he made it through high school so well. He responded, "You let me dream my dream and taught me how Jesus can be in the center of the dream."

Brock sees football as his platform to speak of Christ, and prayer as the legs holding the platform up. Now he is being used to encourage other young people. Brock is now the starting quarterback on his college team, and last week after he tied a school passing record, a reporter stopped him and asked for an interview. Brock said, "Can you stand right here? See, I am leading my team in a prayer at the 50-yard line first. Then I would be glad to answer any questions you might have."

Then he took a few steps and knelt to pray with his team.

As moms, one of the first things we try to do, besides praying for our children ourselves, is to teach them to pray. When we see how God answers their prayers as well as ours, it is truly a blessing.

∿ Meredith, Mop-Heads, and the Leather Coat ∿

BY LANA FLETCHER, CHEHALIS, WASHINGTON

I was making dinner after coming home from church, when my 14-year-old daughter, Meredith, flopped into a chair and announced, "Everyone at church has a leather jacket!"

I looked at her and asked, "Everyone?"

"Well, Jody and Heather do. I've got to have one, Mom."

"Why do you need another coat? You've got your jean jacket, your long dress coat, and your ski jacket." I emphasized the fact by counting off on my fingers. "Your Dad insisted on buying me a leather coat when we were first married," I told her. "It was black and stiff like a straitjacket. It made me feel cold. I finally gave it away because I never wore it."

Meredith kicked off her black heels and pounded up the stairs to her bedroom. She changed out of her church clothes and, as I later found out, she called on God to help her find a way to buy that leather jacket.

The following Tuesday, my daughter and I went shopping. As we walked down Market Boulevard, I pointed in the window of the Country Crafts store and said, "Look, that doll is made out of a mop. I would love to hang it in the laundry room." One look at the price tag convinced me otherwise. It cost 40 dollars. Then I mused out loud, "Too bad I'm not crafty or I'd make one."

Meredith mulled my comment around in her head while we shopped for more practical items. She was crafty and knew she could make a mop doll if she had directions. The very next week in the church foyer she overheard Cindy, an adult church member, talking about learning to make mop dolls. Meredith couldn't believe her good fortune. "My mom wants a mop doll, but they cost too much," she whispered to Cindy. "I'd like to make her one."

"I'll teach you," Cindy volunteered. "Have your dad bring you over tomorrow. I have a wide assortment of colored ribbons and flowers. It will cost you two dollars and fifty cents for the mop head."

At home, Meredith hid the mop doll until Mother's Day. Her handmade gift was a great surprise. I loved it and showed it to everyone, including Mrs. Givens, the Avon lady, who asked, "Would you make three for me, Meredith?"

A look of surprise registered on my daughter's face. "I guess so, if you think I could do them good enough," she answered.

"I'd be glad to pay you," Mrs. Givens said.

Two weeks later, I saw Meredith watching out the window for the Avon lady to arrive. When Mrs. Givens saw the dolls, she said, "These are wonderful. I can hardly wait to give them to my three daughters. They'll love them."

That night Meredith watched out the window again, this time for her dad. She could hardly wait to tell him her good news. "I sold three mop dolls today and made 30 dollars after paying my tithe and paying Mom back for supplies."

"All right!" her dad grinned and hugged her.

"Could I try to sell some dolls at your office?" she begged, excited about the money she had made from her first sale.

"Sure. Then I can retire and you can support me, you'll be so rich," he laughed proudly.

A week later, the Vacation Bible School leader asked Meredith to bring supplies and teach the junior craft class how to make mop dolls. The store, however, was sold out of mops. I am usually thrifty, but the crestfallen look on my daughter's face touched my heart. "I would like to order a case of mops. How soon can it be here?" I asked the clerk.

In a few days, Meredith had plenty of mop heads. Each case had fifty mops. I watched her work day after day, only taking a break to drive the riding lawn mower over the acre of our grass that never stopped growing. She pitched sale after sale to every person she knew. Plus she gave a few dolls as gifts to her grandma, her sister, and her best friend.

After a while, Meredith got tired of making dolls. It was no longer fun to be crafty. She complained that her usually soft, nimble hands felt like they had arthritis. Her hair felt stringy like a mop, and she was sure her eyes were crossed.

"You can't quit now," I insisted. "I'm not going to be stuck with half a case of mops."

I wasn't being hard-hearted, just practical. Finally the last mop was transformed into a doll and sold. Meredith counted her money in the privacy of her bedroom. She had 200 dollars.

"Mom, can you take me shopping?" she asked, running down the stairs.

"Where do you want to go?" I asked, not knowing how much money she had accumulated or what she wanted to do with it.

"To the outlet mall, where the Leather Loft is," she announced triumphantly.

No doubt she could already smell the leather and feel its softness. I had forgotten all about the leather jacket and was surprised to learn that she had been working to earn enough money to purchase the coat. Yet I couldn't help smiling.

We walked into the Leather Loft. Meredith went straight to the rack where the leather jacket was hanging. She removed it from the rack and carried it to the sales counter. The total was 213 dollars. Meredith had forgotten about the tax! Her face looked pale until she saw me smile and reach in my purse. I gladly paid the extra money.

It was August, but despite the summer heat, Meredith wore her leather coat on the drive home. We had both had prayers answered. After 14 years of praying to be a wise mother, I finally felt like one. My daughter had learned that achieving a goal took perseverance and patience. In the process, she also learned that sometimes God's yes answers involve hours and hours of hard work.

When our own moms pray for certain things, we as children, might not always understand our mothers' reasoning or their goals. But when the Lord answers their prayers, we finally see exactly what our moms wanted.

⌁ *All Things Work Together for Good* ⌁

BY JESSIE ANN MOSER, WESCOSVILLE, PENNSYLVANIA

My mother sat across from me in a restaurant booth, mapping out the floor plan of the home I might need someday. She knew her life was almost over and wanted to make sure her husband, my father, would be cared for when she was gone. He had been suffering with Parkinson's disease, and my husband and I were preparing to take him in. One obstacle, Mom was quick to point out, was that we lived in a two-story town home.

"You'll need a ground-floor bedroom and bathroom." Mom pointed at her rough sketch on the restaurant napkin. "And it would be nice to have the family room on the ground floor, too."

It was a strange conversation to be having with my mother, a bit disconcerting, but she was adamant and would not change the subject until she was satisfied that I knew exactly what her desires were.

My mother believed strongly in prayer and God's direction, but was also insistent about providing for the future. She and Dad had already purchased their funeral plots and prepaid their funeral expenses. I remember the day she called me, long before she was diagnosed with cancer, inviting me to celebrate their selection and purchase of two decorative headstones.

"Excuse me. I hope you won't think me too rude." A gray-haired lady with a kind face stood smiling next to our booth, holding out a business card. "I heard you say you might be looking for a new home."

"You heard right," I said, holding up the napkin Mom had been drawing on. "My mom is planning ahead," I said, sparing the woman the details. Mom's thin frame and jaundiced complexion may have already given away our circumstances.

"Well, when you're ready, I hope you'll give my granddaughter Lisa a call," she said. "She's a Realtor and a wonderful girl. I know she'll help you." She handed me the card, and a pretty blond smiled at me from under the company's logo. I thanked her and put the card in my purse.

Our breakfast that spring was one of the last times my mother visited me in Allentown. Mom gave up on chemotherapy and opted for hospice care in her own home. She died in July of that year.

The blond Realtor's business card regularly resurfaced. She smiled at me when I pulled out my credit cards, and every time I looked for my supermarket club card, she was there. Eventually I took her out of my purse and tucked the card into the corner of my dresser mirror.

The heartbreak of losing Mom furthered complications of my dad's Parkinson's disease, so my husband and I began our earnest search for a new home. Moving into Dad's house was out of the question. I remembered the napkin with Mom's rough floor plan, retrieved the Realtor's card from my bedroom, and dialed the number.

Lisa was great, just as her grandmother had said she would be. She showed us over 60 homes, but we could not seem to find exactly the right one. Along with the ground-floor bedroom and bath, my daughter Jessica, a four-year-old at the time, wanted a swimming pool.

After hearing about our months of looking, the receptionist in the realty office approached our agent. The receptionist overheard Lisa and her business partner talking about our search one day. "Maybe my house would work for Jessie." She and her husband had been fixing up their home and were ready to sell and build their dream house.

The house was perfect and in move-in condition. It had a ground-floor bedroom, a full ground-floor bath, and a den right next to Dad's room. And Jessica got her wish: a swimming pool.

I know we would not have found the house without my mother's prayers. She had to be overheard by a kind stranger, a business card would need to be saved for two years, and a receptionist in the Realtor's office had to be ready to sell her home at the exact moment it was needed. I wouldn't call these coincidences, but God-incidences. God answered my precious mother's prayers, establishing His plan from the moment we stepped foot into the restaurant one beautiful spring day, years ago. God works all things together for good, just as He promises.

Dad lived comfortably with our family for three years before he passed away. He often talked about that day in the restaurant with Mom, and now I keep her experiences alive by writing about her. My mother did not fear death; she planned for it. Mom believed in the promise of a place prepared for her, teaching me to do the same. The goal of her prayer was the comfort and care of her family beyond her passing, and God answered through the kindness of a gray-haired stranger with a business card.

4
Family Ties

Prayers for family members and dear friends must be the most plentiful to rise to the throne of God. When our loved ones have a need, we also have a need.

Being a mom is a 24/7 job. The pay can be lousy, the hours exhausting, and often the sacrifices unrecognized. But ask a mom when she's holding her newborn, or when her toddler plants a sticky kiss on the cheek, if it is worth it, and most will answer with a resounding yes! Even when the teenage years hit and Mom wonders where that sweet, lovable child went, she would still do it all again (including the 30 hours of labor) just to hear, "I love you, Mom."

Not everyone has a mom like that, though. So when we can bend our knees and lift up those whom God brings into our lives, we moms might possibly be standing in the gap in more ways than we know. Extended family members, the friends our children bring home—all of them have a story. We may be the only one to let them know their story can have a happy ending.

Therefore, as we have opportunity, let us do good to all people,
especially to those who belong to the family of believers.

Galatians 6:10

There comes a point in our children's lives where we know it is all up to them and God. When we have done all we can physically do to help, that is when all we can do is pray for the Lord to reach them.

⌣ P.S....Pray ⌣

BY SUSAN FARR FAHNCKE, KAYSVILLE, UTAH

Dear Son,

We all miss you. My heart aches with the knowledge that your choices have led you down this awful road that ended in a detention facility. I would do anything to fix your life for you, but I know that only you and the Lord can do that. I pray your time there will help you understand that real happiness can only come from doing what is right. Please know we love you and are praying for you.

Love, Mom
P.S....Pray

My tears blurred the words on the page before me. In all honesty, I didn't know what to say, didn't know what to do that could fix things. The mother in me wanted to just make it all better, but I knew this was something I couldn't fix. My 16-year-old son would have to do this on his own, with God's forgiveness and help.

I had not slept in so long. Exhaustion became normal as deep-rooted anxiety kept me agonizing and praying for my child. He was lost and very far off the path he needed to be on. My pain was so all-encompassing, it felt a lot like grief. I guess in a way it was grief—for the son I once knew, whom I could no longer see.

Big blue-green eyes, filled with mischief and humor, my thoughtful, kind little boy grew to be a teenager I never dreamed he would be. His choices brought him to a darker and darker way of living. I watched as he changed before my eyes, becoming unhappy, angry, and spiraling steadily downward. It was tearing our family apart, tearing my heart to shreds. I felt an overwhelming sense of guilt that I had made mistakes in raising him that brought him to this kind of life. Now all I could do to reach him was to make occasional visits and send mail, which they allowed him to read, then took away.

Each day I began a new letter, tucking it into a card with a funny joke or a spiritual message. I prayed hard to know what to say, to know what my Father in heaven would have me tell my son that would make a difference. With each letter I felt inadequate in my words, but I always ended with the same postscript: P.S….Pray.

I received one letter from my son while he was incarcerated.

> Dear Mom,
>
> I am so sorry for all the things I've done. I miss you all so much and I can't wait to get out of here to start over. I am reading my scriptures every day and I think this has been good for me. I needed to be here. I can't wait to come home.
>
> P.S….I'm praying.

Eventually he was released and given probation. When he came home, my son had a new light in his eyes. He seemed focused and happy and appreciative. We welcomed him with open arms, and soon his life was back on track.

And then he started slipping back into his old lifestyle again. At first it was little things, breaking small rules and charming his way out of things. But as time went on, I saw his whole countenance changing again. He looked *dark*—there is no other way to describe it. His choices were allowing Satan to rule his life, and once again I knew he was very far off the path.

And so it went. For over a year, my child slipped back and forth, in and out of trouble, each time with consequences that I hoped would be enough of a learning experience that he would finally *learn*. And each time he was in trouble, I prayed from the depth of my soul for some way to reach him, to help him. Time and again I received the feeling that my son had to do this himself. All I could do was love him as Christ loves him: unconditionally. I repeatedly told him how much I loved him and how much God loves him and how that would never, ever change.

I know prayer is the one thing I can do for him. I pray with him, I pray for him, and I gently prompt him to pray.

I watch him struggle. It's like watching someone trying to swim for the first time and not being able to help. When he surfaces, I can see the light in his eyes, the hope and happiness that come from living the way God wants us to. I pray harder and try to keep close with him, so that he never doubts my love.

One day we were talking about his time in detention. I asked him what it was like, and he said it was one part like hell and one part like heaven. I asked him how on earth it could ever be like heaven, and he said that with no distractions, nothing to do but read Scripture and pray, it brought him closer to God than at any other time in his life. He told me how my letters made him so homesick, but he always looked for my little postscript, and it was like his compass: *P.S.... Pray.*

We take it day by day now. We end each day with prayer as a family. I have definite hope that he will make it. He has so much good, so much potential to one day be a great man who walks with the Lord. He still makes mistakes, but one thing is constant throughout his life: the power of prayer.

It is the thing I know makes a difference and the certain way to find the right path. It was the answer to my prayers for my child, the direction God gave me. It's not the answer I thought I was looking for, but it's the one God gave me.

We pray.

A mom's sudden need to pray for her child can happen at any minute, even without the child being present. Anne simply knew she needed to pray, and pray she did. It was "God-spiration," and she learned that day to never ignore her intuition again.

~ An Urge to Pray ~

BY ANNE CULBREATH WATKINS, VINEMONT, ALABAMA

"I love you, too, Mom." I was just putting the Closed sign on the door while chatting with Laura, my daughter, on the telephone. I took every opportunity I had to speak with her. Her schedule with college, work, and other activities gave us only a few short minutes every day. But she enjoyed her active life and assured me that everything was fine. She went to school in the morning and then to work at a hotel desk job, where she handled the second shift, six nights a week.

I worried about her while she was working, knowing that a second shift alone could be dangerous. I continuously kept her in my prayers, asking the Lord to protect her.

"Have a good night at work and be careful, honey." I hung up the phone, rounded up my belongings, and headed out the door to my car.

I always enjoyed the 25-minute drive home to the country. My husband, Allen, and I loved the peacefulness of our home's location, even if it meant a further commute. Winding my way through the meandering roads gave me time to relax after a long day at work.

Tonight was different, though. Not more than five miles from home, an overwhelming sense of dread pressed me. "Oh God, I don't know what's wrong. I don't know who I am praying for, but I'm asking You to watch over my loved ones." I had just spoken with Laura, so I was sure everything was fine with her.

"Is it Allen, Lord?" I drove as fast as I dared on the twisting, rural roads, and as soon as I reached home, I dialed his cell phone.

"Hi, honey. I am doing just fine, just working late tonight." Even with Allen's reassurance, the nauseating sense of apprehension still lingered.

I continued praying with urgency. I just couldn't shake the feeling that something terrible was going to happen.

Sometime later, I glanced at the clock. *Ten minutes before eleven, nearly time for Laura to finish her shift for the night.* I asked God to keep her safe as she drove home to her apartment and went to bed.

The phone startled my husband and me from our sleep, and I heard Allen gasp after he answered. "Are you all right?" The tone of his voice sent shivers racing through my body. He handed me the phone. "It's Laura."

I snatched the receiver and cried, "What's wrong?"

"Mom!" Laura's normally cheery voice sounded strained. "I was robbed at gunpoint by two men."

At just about the time I had checked my clock, Laura was counting the cash drawer, getting it organized for the next shift. While gathering her things to go home, the front door opened and two men came to the front desk.

Laura greeted them as she would any other customers, but what happened next could have been a scene from a bad movie. "Mom, one of them pointed a shotgun right at my face, and the other one jumped over my desk and shoved me toward the register." I heard her breaking into tears. "I just threw my hands into the air and cried out to God for help. They told me to shut up and just give them the money."

"Oh, Laura..." My eyes filled with tears as I listened to my daughter spill her story.

"I just couldn't make the register drawer open, Mom. I was so scared! So the man behind the counter shoved me aside and started punching keys until it opened. There wasn't very much in there, Mom. I had just cleaned out the drawer and put most of it in an envelope. I told him that and, in fact, it was sitting right on the counter." Laura grew quieter. "I thought they were going to kill me."

I held back the flood of emotion I was feeling. "Honey, what happened next?"

"Instead of grabbing the money, he pushed past me and vaulted over the front desk. Both of the men ran out of the lobby and sped away in a waiting car." I could hear the trembling in my daughter's voice. "Mom, I cried out to God that they wouldn't hurt me, and they didn't!"

I remembered the sickening dread that filled me earlier, prompting me to prayer. My daughter was safe, and God showed me that He answers mothers' prayers, even when we don't know for whom we are praying!

When a mom's child is soon to be a mother herself, prayers are quickly spoken. Shirley knew they had to pray for the Lord to solve the problem, and He didn't let them down.

◡∶ *Mom, I'm Pregnant* ∶◠

BY SHIRLEY ROSE, AURORA, ILLINOIS

Vanessa, my teenaged daughter, handed me a folded piece of paper. She was unable to say the words out loud, and had chosen instead to write them. *Mom, I'm pregnant.* Tears poured down her face as I read the rest of the letter. There was an apology from both Vanessa and her boyfriend, Greg. She asked for support from her father and me, but she would understand if we never spoke to her again.

How can I explain my feelings? My unmarried, 17-year-old daughter was pregnant. I visualized all the hopes and dreams and promise and possibility for her life slipping away. It was like being hit in the chest with a two-by-four. I couldn't breathe. I didn't know if I should cry, scream, hug her, or crumple to the floor.

I sat in stunned silence. Vanessa spoke first. "Mom, we didn't mean for this to happen, but it *has* happened. And if we don't want this baby, the baby will know. We can't reject him."

How typical of Vanessa to be thinking of the baby, even now. What could I say to her? As devastated and angry as I was, her wise words about the baby took the fight right out of me. I put my arms around her and assured her that we *would* want this baby, though he or she certainly deserved a better beginning. I asked one very important question: "What are you going to do about God? You are obviously not serving Him."

"We want to make things right with God," she answered. "We've asked God to forgive us. Will you please forgive us, Mom?"

In hindsight, I should have seen it coming. The warning signs were in place. Vanessa and Greg were too close and together far too often. By the time they were 17 and 18 years of age, they had been dating for two and a half years. Vanessa had given up most of her friends to spend more time with Greg. They were inseparable. There were times when my husband, Jerry, and I tried to keep them apart, but they always managed to thwart our attempts. We felt powerless to divert their escalating relationship. When they talked about marriage, we put off their questions and gave the usual pat answers: "You have plenty of time. You both need to focus on getting an education."

During the time they dated, Jerry and I came to love Greg as our own son. His parents divorced, and his father moved to another state. His childhood home was sold. It was painful for him to stay in a small apartment with his mother, brother, and sister. Outside of work and school, he spent almost every waking moment at our home. Jerry had become a father figure to him. Greg was a wonderful person, but far too young and ill-prepared to be a father.

When Vanessa was breaking the news of her pregnancy to me, Greg was with Jerry, giving him the same news. Jerry was speaking at a church that night. Greg showed up in a pitiful state. He hadn't eaten or slept in three days. He faced the most difficult task of his life: to tell the man he respected most in the world how completely he had let him down.

After the service, Greg made his way to the front of the church. Jerry reached out, put his hand on the young man's shoulder, and said, "Greg, I want you to know, you're like my own son."

It was the worst thing Jerry could have said to him. "Can we go somewhere and talk?" he asked.

Greg told Jerry he had done something he had promised he would never do. He had gotten Vanessa pregnant. He had broken his word. He had betrayed Jerry's trust and let him down. When Greg finished talking, he braced himself for Jerry's reaction.

"You're right," said Jerry. "You *have* betrayed my trust. You've disappointed me terribly. What do you plan to do?"

"Vanessa and I want to be married as soon as possible. We want to provide a loving, Christian home for our child."

"That's just fine," spat Jerry, "but you're not qualified to do anything but flip hamburgers. How do you think you can support a wife and child?"

"I don't know, but I'll do whatever I have to do," replied Greg.

The four of us sat and talked for several hours that evening. Jerry and I worked our way through anger and disappointment. The dreams and plans for our daughter's future were shattered. Vanessa and Greg asked for our forgiveness. Eventually we gave it and moved forward.

We all fail God. Some sins are just more visible than others. We had to think of the baby. This was our grandchild, an innocent who deserved a good start in life. We were left with one overwhelming question and prayer: "God, how can we handle this matter in a way that brings honor and glory to Your name, not reproach?"

A pregnant, unmarried teenage daughter is a challenge for any family. Vanessa's pregnancy was especially difficult for us. Jerry is a minister and a recognized television personality. Many people would be watching to see how we handled the situation.

The questions seemed overwhelming. Should we give Vanessa and Greg a church wedding or a quiet, private ceremony? Would our pastor be willing to marry them? If we had a wedding, how could we pull it off in three weeks? Whom should we invite? How should we tell our staff, our friends, our families? Would it be a sin for Vanessa to wear a wedding dress? Should her dress be white? How could we demonstrate forgiveness and support to our kids without appearing to minimize or excuse their sin? It was a huge dilemma.

Greg and Vanessa asked for nothing more than a quiet ceremony in the pastor's office. It made us want to give them as much as we could, without stepping over the line. But where *was* the line? I went to God in earnest prayer. "Lord," I agonized, "how do we get through this and still please You? We want to give Vanessa and Greg a wedding for many reasons. She is our only daughter. This baby deserves a good beginning. If they are to be married anyway, can it be a nice little church wedding? How, Lord? How?"

I have never experienced such a sudden and obvious answer to prayer. An idea came to me. Vanessa and Greg could write a letter and put it in each wedding invitation. They could explain their situation right up front. That way no one would feel like we had tried to hide anything. The idea seemed like a possible solution, but it had to be Vanessa and Greg's decision.

I was pleasantly surprised by their reaction. "I had already planned to write a letter to my family members," Greg said. "I hadn't thought of sending it with the wedding invitations." Vanessa agreed that it would be a good way to handle things. We all believed it was a solution from God in direct answer to my prayer. The following is the letter we drafted together:

> Dear Family and Friends,
>
> You may be surprised by this invitation, and it deserves an explanation.
>
> We have been going together for over two years and we love each other very much. We had planned to get married in about a year. However, we have decided to move the wedding date to December 17 because we are expecting a baby.
>
> This is very difficult to share with you because you are special to us. Though we had determined to keep our relationship pure, we made a serious mistake and we are now faced with the consequences of our sin. We offer no excuses. We have sincerely repented and asked God to forgive us. We have also asked for our parents' forgiveness, and now we ask for yours.
>
> We want to present ourselves before God in marriage so that our lives together can have His blessing. This is important for us and for our child.
>
> We want our wedding to be a time of joy and celebration of our lives together, and of God's mercy and grace to all of us. We hope you can share this day with us. If not, we would still ask for your prayers and blessing.
>
> Love,
> Vanessa and Greg

We expected some negative responses from the letter, but received only positive ones. If anyone disapproved, we don't know about it to this day.

It was a small, but beautiful wedding, bathed in God's presence. Through answered prayer, He showed us how to handle a difficult situation, and we were able to bring honor and glory to His name.

> Not only can a mom's prayer for her son be answered, but the Lord can also use it to answer someone else's prayer. We never know how the effects of fervent prayer can trickle down, touching lives and hearts.

∿ Mine Story ∿

BY CARLETA FERNANDES, AMARILLO, TEXAS

"MeeMaw, MeeMaw, tell *mine* story." My five-year-old darling climbed onto my lap. He never tired of hearing "mine story."

"Once upon a time in a faraway land called Kansas, there was an itty-bitty baby boy. He was so tiny, I do not think he even had a name," I began.

Grinning, he snuggled closer to me, fragrant from his bath. "Did too. Did too. It's Ryan. That's me!"

I watched his pale-blue eyes close briefly as he yawned, unsure whether he could stay awake until "...and they lived happily ever after."

As I began to tell Ryan his story, my thoughts were on his real story—the one I could not tell him. Ryan was the product of a too-early marriage of a violent young man and an immature girl. The situation was so bad for his mother, Katie, that she divorced the father before Ryan was born. His father became an unknown ghost from their distant past, never to make contact again.

In 1976, my son, Robert, met Katie through mutual friends. It was not long before Katie and Ryan became a constant presence in our household. We loved and spoiled the tiny newborn. However, Katie and Robert's friendship seemed casual, and they soon became involved with other people.

The next year my job in Kansas ended. We closed the wonderful old house in Lawrence and returned to our hometown in Texas, leaving Katie and Ryan behind as well.

After Robert left, Katie was distraught. She missed him painfully. Maybe the friendship wasn't as casual as she had thought. Katie struggled to continue on without Robert and to simply survive. She had no family and few stable friends to help her.

Katie was vulnerable. She met an unsavory character who was in town visiting his brother in nearby Leavenworth Federal Penitentiary. Out of the need to be loved, Katie quickly fell for the handsome man. With promises of marriage, home, and prosperity, Mike persuaded Katie to bring little Ryan and relocate to a small town in northern Nebraska.

But Mike had a malicious and jealous nature. The violence and control Katie's first husband had over her was nothing in comparison to the situation she was in now. Near-poverty, beatings, and servitude seemed to be her lot in life. Katie and Ryan lived in terror, with no one to turn to.

Determined to survive, Katie hid small change, sometimes only pennies and nickels. When she had a chance, she returned items to the grocery store for cash after Mike had checked the receipts and money spent. She saved every bit she could. Someday there would be a way out.

"Please, dear God, help me," Katie prayed every night.

Katie thought often of Robert: his gentle kindness and his slow, sweet smile. She knew he was in Texas, but where? She had no idea.

She couldn't stop thinking of the sweet, gentle man who was still in both her and Ryan's heart.

One afternoon Katie was putting away Ryan's toys. In the bottom of the toy chest, she saw a football—the kind cheerleaders throw out to the crowds at football games. Picking it up, she remembered the day Robert had given it to Ryan—one of those remarkable days with a picnic at the river and a drive afterward.

She knew Robert's two sisters had been cheerleaders in his hometown in Texas. On the football was a telephone number and the name of a bank. As an idea formed in her mind, she spoke a prayer of hope.

The next day was laundry day. Katie pulled off extra bedding. She gathered up several other things, too—items that did not really require washing. She needed to add to her small stash of change. Mike counted the loads.

Grumbling about the extra laundry, he handed over the exact amount of money Katie told him she needed. He took her to the Laundromat and would pick her up in two hours.

Quickly sorting the clothes, she changed all the money into quarters, started the machines, and went to the pay phone on the wall. She had an important call to make.

"First State Bank," the girl answered.

"I, ah, need to, umm, ask a question. Do you know a guy named Robert Duran?"

"Sure, I went to school with Robert."

Katie was shaking. "Can you tell me if he has any family in town?"

"Well, yes, but I saw him this morning at the café. He's working for his dad in the machine shop. I can give you that number if you'd like."

Katie couldn't believe the friendliness in the girl's voice. How could she be so helpful to a stranger on the phone? Since Katie wasn't one to question such good fortune too closely, she thanked the banker while jotting down the number. Before she lost her nerve, she began to dial.

Her stack of quarters was so small. "Please be enough," she prayed.

"Machine shop," a man answered. It was Robert. She had found him.

Between sobs her story spilled out. "Oh, Robert, I need help."

Robert got the number to the laundry and called her back. Robert had missed Katie, too, and thought she and little Ryan were gone from his life forever. Plans were made for Robert to call again at the same time in one week. By the end of the conversation, they were both in tears.

Two weeks later, struggling to carry Ryan most of the way, Katie walked three long, dusty miles to a short dirt airstrip. Robert was waiting for them in his father's Citabria airplane. Since the plane was a small two-seat aerobatics aircraft, there was little space. Ryan would ride on Katie's lap.

With room for only one small bag, most of their belongings were left behind. Katie knew this was a small sacrifice for the relief from danger and fear under which they had been living.

God heard Katie's prayers.

Ryan held fast to the small First State Bank football, now his favorite toy, as Robert sped down the runway. They were on their way to a brighter future.

"...and they lived happily ever after." I glanced down. Ryan's long, blond lashes lay softly on his cheek. He was sound asleep, still curled warmly, safely on my lap.

At long last, Ryan was beginning to feel truly at home after an early childhood of chaos, danger, and uncertainty. Now he was safe. PeePaw, MeeMaw, and Robert, his new daddy, would keep him that way. He was now sleeping through the night after several years of nightmares, bed-wetting, and behavior problems.

"Yes," I thought to myself as I tucked Ryan into bed, "God does answer prayers." I have a beautiful daughter-in-law and a wonderful grandson. Ryan and Katie have a family that loves them. My sweet, shy Robert is happy once more.

"Mine story" belongs to each of us.

> It sometimes takes a long time for children to reap the benefits of unsolicited prayer on their behalf, given by their parents. But when the answers come, they are powerful indeed.

The Power of Praying Parents

BY DR. DEBRA PEPPERS, ST. LOUIS, MISSOURI

"I will be the captain of team A, but let's get 'fatty' to be the captain for team B." I didn't realize he was referring to me until my classmates started pushing me to the front of the room. Everyone was laughing. The teacher, Mrs. Buchanan, reprimanded him; but at the tender age of eight, I experienced my first real humiliation. Forty years and hundreds of derogatory remarks later, I still recall that painful incident.

Growing up in Clarkson, Missouri, in the 1960s should have been easy, and was for most children. The community was upright and innocent, a picturesque town situated along the banks of the Mississippi. The population hovered around 500 residents, and everyone knew everyone else.

I often heard neighbors say, "That nice Duvall family. You know, they own half the town. The grandfather, Milton, he served in

Congress, and his wife is a pillar of the church. The parents, well, they're model citizens, involved in everything. That family has it all…except for poor Debbie."

I heard that name applied to me many times. And why not? My sister, Donna, was my hero and role model. She was four years older and was everything I wanted to be: head cheerleader, prom queen, valedictorian, and yearbook queen. My younger brother, Duke, was a star athlete, student council representative, and Mr. Popularity. A handsome young man, he oozed charm and charisma. Then there was "poor Debbie."

I learned in the fifth grade that if I got into trouble before recess, I wouldn't be allowed to go outside. Instead I could remain under the watchful eye of the janitor while he cleaned the cafeteria, and it became a haven of sorts to me. As long as I was inside during recess, I wouldn't have to face ridicule on the outside.

One day I confessed to my teacher why I was always in trouble, and she allowed me to spend my lunch recess in the room, helping her grade papers. That's when I learned to cheat, changing *D*'s to *A*'s in the grade book.

By seventh grade, I had lost all semblance of a conscience. During my teen years, I progressed to genuine hostility and indifference. I intimidated my classmates and found pride in knowing my peers were afraid of me. My parents were afraid of what I might become. The tougher I became, the better my "friends" liked me.

As my grades and self-worth continued to plummet, I gave up competing with my sister. It was much easier getting attention by being the class clown.

In high school I drowned my sorrows in food, and at 100 pounds overweight, my self-esteem was nonexistent. I did what I could to mask my insecurities. Harmful actions gave me a sense of power. I cussed at my teachers and fought with anyone remotely interested. I drank, smoked, sniffed, or swallowed anything to ease my pain. And because of me, my family became the talk of the town.

My parents worked hard and provided a loving home for their children, but rearing me entailed more drudgery than joy. They sent me to counselors and doctors, and every time I was in trouble, they were there to rescue me, trying everything humanly possible to pull me from my path of self-destruction.

Because my parents watched me so closely, I had to devise places to hide my stash of party supplies that had progressed from food to other "highs." I made a copy of the family car key and began sneaking out regularly. A friend taught me to roll back the odometer so my dad wouldn't know I had stolen the car.

The last time I ran away from home, I didn't discover the freedom I sought, rather I found how ill-prepared for life I actually was. A prodigal child, I returned home. Though my parents welcomed me warmly, the rules had changed, and I could stay home only if I agreed to abide by their terms.

Twenty years and a college education later, I received a gift from my parents. When I opened the box, I found a letter from my dad. He had written it just before I ran away that last time, but I had not seen it until now. I opened it carefully and wept like a baby as I read the following:

> January 1968
>
> My Darling Baby Girl,
>
> I write this because you have threatened to run away again and I am leaving it on your pillow with hopes that you will get it before you leave. I know at seventeen you're a young woman and we can't stop you from going. Your mom and I have asked ourselves a thousand times where we went wrong…where we failed you. I would give anything if we could go back to the days when you were Daddy's little girl, snuggling up on my lap and bringing all your hurts to me to make them better. I only blame myself for all that has gone wrong and would give my

very life for a chance to make it right. I didn't see how much you were hurting. Mommy and I have prayed continuously for you, asking God if we were too strict or too lenient, and what we can do to make everything all right for you. Dearest Debbie Girl, we love you with no strings attached. God brought you to us and no matter what, you will always be my precious baby girl. When you read this, no matter how late, please come talk to me.

Always,
Your Loving Daddy

I knew my parents had prayed for me, but didn't realize until that moment how God had answered them. They supported me in my endeavors to become a teacher, and I spent 30 years reaching out to every "problem child," considering each of these children a diamond in the rough. As horrible and painful as my adolescence was, it gave me an invaluable perspective on life and on young people. Because of my parents' prayers, I have been privileged to advise hundreds of parents and teens enduring severe emotional problems, eventually launching the Crisis Intervention Team and Alternative School in my district. Because of my personal experience, God has used me to help guide parents and youth workers in mentoring kids struggling through difficult times—kids written off as hopeless.

As a radio talk-show host in St. Louis, I am an advocate for troubled kids.

I am also a motivational speaker, and my parents often travel with me. One event stands out in my memory. A few years back, I was invited to be the keynote speaker at a women's conference at the Crystal Cathedral. My parents were seated at the back of the audience, and after I presented my story, the crowd simultaneously stood and applauded. However, the ovation was not for me. It was for my parents.

There are two special things my parents did for me, and they include these in their advice to other people: First, no matter how bleak the situation, see it through the eyes of faith. And second, never stop praying. Thank you, Mom and Dad, for your unconditional love, and thank You, Lord, for the gift of answered prayer.

Dee knew the doctors had to be wrong. She just knew it. So she prayed and God listened.

Heaven's Special Child

BY DEE SMITH, HOUSTON, TEXAS

My husband, Jim, and I sat across from the psychologist. We were waiting for him to tell us the results of our four-year-old daughter's battery of tests from the previous day. He was stacking and shuffling papers. The only other noise in the room was the tick, tick, tick of an antique grandfather clock. It sounded like a time bomb to me. I tried to distract my anxious mind by studying the doctor.

He had a kind face, wore horn-rimmed glasses, and looked like the wise old owl in a Disney movie. He cleared his throat and said, "Mr. and Mrs. Smith, it seems as if your daughter's problem is not a hearing loss as we suspected, but a…" A harsh, loud, female voice interrupted. "The psychometric testing shows, without a doubt, your daughter is retarded."

My head jerked around to see a tall woman leaning casually against the frame of the open door. One look at her and rage boiled in me. Without thinking, I started to get out of my chair and attack like a bear cub's mama. Jim stood up, grabbed my hand, and pulled me tightly against his side. The psychologist introduced the woman as his wife and colleague. She had conducted most of the testing. The haze in front of my eyes cleared, and what I saw did not make me feel any better. She had short red hair, combed and styled like she had just left the beauty parlor. She wore a pastel-blue pantsuit, expensive and unwrinkled on her slim figure. I felt dowdy and inferior in my best two-piece pink linen suit, already wrinkled from holding a squirming four-year-old, and stained under the arms from nervous perspiration.

I watched her walk to her husband's desk and pick up a folder labeled "SMITH, Vicki Ann," and then sit down in an overstuffed chair adjacent to his desk. She explained the details of the test results, which I couldn't understand or soak in. Her voice assaulted my ears like someone running fingernails across a blackboard. I looked at her husband, hoping this was a mistake.

Our pediatrician didn't find anything wrong with her development in the four years of her life. He had referred us for testing to check for a speech or hearing problem. *Retarded* was like a death sentence to me. Jim, always the practical thinker, asked, "What kind of treatment does she need? Is there some type of special training she requires? Will she be able to go to school?" and so forth. Their answers faded into background noise. I was busy composing a letter of complaint to the head of their facility. Soon, but not soon enough for me, the appointment was over.

Jim and I walked to the parking lot, each locked into our own thoughts. We had been married five years—long enough for me to know that he had to think things through to a nice, neat solution. As for me, I didn't believe a word the doctors said. Doctors can be wrong. We needed a second opinion.

I barely noticed the newly mowed lawns and fresh flowers lining the sidewalks. The cloudless sky and light breeze made a mockery of my misery. I fought back tears and a painful lump in my throat. "If

this is true, she's better off dead!" I blurted out to no one in particular, maybe to God. There was no answer from my husband or God.
I could hardly believe I had uttered those awful words.

That evening, as I gave Vicki a bath, I looked over every inch of
her body to see if I had missed something—some flaw or physical
sign. Her eyes were bright-blue. She squealed and giggled when I
poured a cup of water over her head. When we were done, she stood
up and reached out for me to pick her up, asking for a cookie. I said
no, and she hugged my neck a little tighter and said, "Pwease,
Mommy. Cookie? I good girl." *There is nothing wrong with her brain.
So what if she only knows a few words. A lot of babies talk late. She is perfectly normal and can do a lot of normal things. The doctors are wrong.*

I could write volumes on the anguish I experienced over the next
ten years. I prayed. I pleaded. I yelled in anger at God's silence. Jim
worried a lot and worked hard to make sure Vicki received the best
medical tests, training, and specialists money could buy. She was
wired, medicated, X-rayed, stuck with needles, and probed by white-
jacketed strangers. One day a doctor looked up from Vicki's thick
medical folder and said frankly, "Mrs. Smith, my recommendation is
for placement into an institution that provides special care for children like your daughter."

"No! I will never do that to her," I shouted. "We will take care of
her." In my denial, bitterness, and ignorance of God's ways, I fought
everyone and everything that would help us. My marriage unraveled,
I broke down emotionally and physically, and I neglected my two
"normal" sons. Most of my time was spent *pushing* Vicki to learn at
a pace too difficult for her. God seemed so far away, even when we
went to church. All I could see was a "professional opinion" based on
tests from the scientific knowledge available in 1964.

God was near. We just didn't know it. He was working behind
the scenes, moving hearts, opening doors of discovery for medical
science, and waiting for us to keep in touch with Him by prayer.
While we were slowly building our faith, He was helping Vicki to

grow in hers. God heard our prayers, but answered them in His way and His time.

There have been many heartaches and victories in our family, but Vicki is a visible demonstration of this Scripture verse: "And we know that in all things God works for the good of those who love him, who have been called according to his purpose" (Romans 8:28).

The little girl I once thought might be better off dead is very much alive. She is still pretty, even with gray hair. She likes it that way. She is intellectually challenged in some things, but very good at other things. She has grown up to become a cheerful, friendly, compassionate woman, helping other people who live at a building named "The Center," which is her home.

She loves God, knows about Jesus and the cross, and loves to go to church. She is simple, but I see something wise in her spirit. She loves her family and extended family, including their dogs and cats. She knows her grandpa is in heaven, and that I will go there one day. She knows she is going there, too.

Vicki has a purpose in life. She is our "angel on earth." She is heaven's special child, loaned to us for a while, here to teach *us* the simple and beautiful things in life. She is the visible evidence of God's love for us, her family.

We pray for guidance in raising our children. In order to teach them, sometimes God has to teach us first.

∴ Chocolate Prayers ∾

BY ANA CORMANY, HATFIELD, PENNSYLVANIA

I thought I could protect him. I am his mother, after all. I read the articles and heeded the advice of the authorities. "Keep your computer in a central location, add a filtration device, and talk to your kids about the dangers of porn," the experts warned.

"How did this happen?" I wondered. "Where did I go wrong?" My husband and I sat with our son, Daniel, in our home office on three chairs strategically placed close together in a circle. It was the place where all of our four children sat with us from time to time through the years to discuss individual concerns and to hand out corrections for their childish offensives.

"Daniel, Phil checked the Web history today and discovered an address for a porn site. He told Dad and me because, even though he can tease you unmercifully sometimes, he's your older brother, and he really does care about you."

His once-warm chocolate-brown eyes seemed cold and rigid as he stared at the floor, avoiding our gaze of concern. We waited. Each moment of quietness ticked by slowly and painfully as he struggled for words to express his secret shame, while my mind raced on in silent prayer, crying out to the Lord. *Jesus, please no. This can't be happening!*

I have tried so hard to protect his innocence. I know how addictive porn is! I had seen marriages torn apart when the two, who were meant to be one, died a slow, painful death because porn sliced through their intimacy. It left them staggering away from each other, permanently severed and bleeding profusely. I didn't want that for my son. I wanted him whole, with the ability to one day give himself freely to one woman for a lifetime.

"Please, Jesus, give us the wisdom to guide him through this, and please wipe those poisonous pictures from his precious mind!"

Breaking the silence, he told us that his first exposure to porn occurred months earlier. He and his friends had been playing in the local teenager hangout—just a crude fort built back in the woods in our neighborhood. Hidden there among the empty soda cans and candy wrappers was a pornographic magazine. Recognizing this was the kind of magazine their parents had warned them about, Daniel and his friends decided to destroy it, ripping it into shreds, page by toxic page.

"It's like those pictures got stuck in the back of my mind," he explained as he pointed to the back of his head.

He continued.

"I was alone in the house one day," he confided. "You left to run an errand, Mom. I just couldn't get those pictures out of my mind, so I searched for a Web site."

Oh, Jesus, how stupid we were to let him use our new computer without first installing the filter, I confessed silently to God in prayer. *What can we do? How can we help him?*

I heard the still, small voice enter the chambers of my mind with a firm command: *Give up chocolate for Daniel, Ana.*

What? I don't think I heard You right, God. Give up chocolate? What on earth does that have to do with anything?

My husband once again explained the dangers of porn to our son as a battle continued to rage in my mind.

Chocolate was my passion, my forbidden fruit. My doctor told me to give it up long ago. "The caffeine in chocolate isn't good for you. It's causing some of your symptoms," she warned.

"I eliminated caffeine in all other areas of my diet," I had said to defend myself. "I haven't had caffeine in my sodas or tea in years. But give up chocolate? I will deal with the symptoms, thank you very much!"

And now it wasn't my doctor who was asking me to give up chocolate, but the Holy Spirit, the Great Physician.

Give up chocolate for Daniel? I questioned in my mind. *Give it up for what?*

Temptation. It's about temptation, Ana, the calm, but firm voice explained. *Every time you feel the temptation to eat another piece of chocolate, I want you to pray for Daniel and his temptation to look at porn.*

But Lord, do you know how often that is? I eat chocolate every day in some form or another! You don't understand! It's not that I don't want to do it. I can't! The temptation's too great! I will fail You, and I will fail my son! I can't make a commitment like that!

Finishing his explanation on the dangers of porn, my husband added, "We will be here to help you, Daniel, in any way that we can. From now on, you will not be able to use the new computer until a filtering system is installed. After that, you will have a limit of one hour of computer time each day. We will also be checking with you on a regular basis to see how you're doing in this struggle."

I didn't want to let the words out. I tried to bite my tongue and swallow the words one by one, but my lips began to move out of a greater sense of obedience, and I choked the sentence out one word at a time. "Daniel, I'll make a deal with you." *Oh no! What am I saying?*

"I will give up chocolate for you, and every time I'm tempted to eat it, I'll pray for you and your temptation to look at porn."

My husband, knowing my addiction to chocolate, looked dazed as if to say, "Do you know what you just committed yourself to?" I looked back, frightened by the commitment I had just made, but relieved by my decision to be obedient.

I wasted no time. I knew I would need the prayers of my husband and a few close friends to keep my promise to Daniel. They gladly agreed to pray for me as I began to engage in the biggest battle of my life.

Chocolate was everywhere, and my prayers for Daniel reached the ear of God on a regular basis. I prayed as I passed by the chocolate chips in my cupboard. I prayed at every potluck dinner held at my church. And I prayed in the checkout line at the grocery store and at Wal-Mart.

It was in the checkout line at Wal-Mart that I nearly lost my battle. It was 4:30 in the afternoon, and I had not eaten any lunch. *Where are the Paydays?* I whispered to myself. *Peanuts held together by a caramel center—I can have that,* I thought. But where were they? I searched the aisle desperately and to no avail, when suddenly there they were: pecan turtles—pecans drizzled in caramel and smothered in chocolate. My favorite!

He'll never know, I told myself. *I can throw the wrapper away, and he'll never see it. I'm 38 years old, and if I want to eat chocolate...I'll eat chocolate!*

The advancement of the checkout line awoke me from my thoughts of defiance, and I loaded my items onto the conveyer belt, moping like a child just caught in an act of disobedience...a narrow escape.

As I drove home, I thought of how close I came to indulging in chocolate rather than immersing myself in prayers for my son. When I arrived home, I knew what I needed to do.

"Daniel, there is something I need to confess to you." He looked at me intently, his brown eyes sparkling with the freedom of an innocent child. I told him every detail of my checkout-line experience, and how I had almost given in to the temptation.

"Gee, Mom, I haven't felt the least bit tempted lately," he exclaimed.

My prayers were working. I stood there amazed and overjoyed, realizing that I could try to protect my son by following all of the experts' advice, but nothing would do more to guard my son's heart and mind than the fervent prayers of his mother. And God knew just how to get me to pray on a consistent basis for my son: by trading my temptation for prayers to battle his.

5
Medical Miracles

IT'S DIFFICULT TO SAY which is harder to endure: watching your child suffer with health problems, or seeing your child watch you endure a disability or addiction that keeps you from being the mother you long to be. Thankfully, God understands and has promised His help and compassion. The Bible is filled with stories of miraculous healings. Isaiah 41:13 reminds us that He has our right hand in His. He says not to fear. He promises that He will help us. It's a promise worth clinging to, no matter whose health is in question. God cannot lie, and His Word is so powerful that it created the heavens and the earth. So in spite of how things look (or feel), we can rely on His faithfulness. Just hold on to His hand a little tighter.

Then your light will break forth like the dawn, and your healing
will quickly appear; then your righteousness will go before you,
and the glory of the LORD will be your rear guard.

ISAIAH 58:8

Seeing a child in pain and suffering can grip a mom's heart in icy fear—fear beyond all normal reason. Through prayer Cheri found a way to melt the ice and trust in God.

✑ God Answers a Prayer of Release ✒

BY CHERI FULLER, EDMOND, OKLAHOMA

Dread tied my stomach in knots before I ever opened my eyes that September Sunday morning. Even in deep sleep I listened for the sound that sparked fear in me. The rattling sound was all the scarier because it emanated from the chest of my six-year-old son, Justin.

His skin was pale and drawn, and his chest heaved as he gasped for a breath. I looked into his blue eyes and saw a reflection of my own fears.

Scrambling out of bed, I ran for his inhaler. Asthma had become the embodiment of every fear I owned. I had tried so hard to protect my children, giving them nutritious meals and vitamins, hovering over them like a quail with her covey. My husband, Holmes, thought I was being overprotective, and I knew I was. But how could I explain the horrible dread that welled up in me, especially when our firstborn was sick?

When asthma hit Justin at age four, it had not been a simple case of wheezing. His first attack had been full-blown *status asthmaticus,* and it took days in a hospital to bring his breathing back to normal.

That's what I hated most about asthma: I was powerless to control it. An attack could hit any moment, changing our plans. This chronic illness had stolen my joy and overtaken our lives. It had even curtailed our travel to the grandparents' ranch in Texas because we would wind up in an emergency room due to the climate change.

Just as we always did, we consulted with the doctor on the phone that September day, gave Justin all his medicine, and made sure he used his inhaler and rested. But this time nothing worked. Even with careful nursing, as the day grew longer, his wheezing worsened.

So by 10:00 that night, we dropped our two younger children at a neighbor's and sped to the hospital emergency room in the rain. After several injections of adrenaline and IV medications didn't snap him out of the attack, the emergency room doctor called our pediatrician. When I saw Justin's doctor stride down the long, gray hall, I breathed a sign of relief. *I just know he can get Justin's asthma attack under control. He always has before.*

"Raise the level of aminophyllin and cortisone. Give him another adrenaline injection," he ordered the emergency room nurses. "An asthma attack is like a ball rolling down a hill," Dr. Spencer told us. "We've got to stop it with the biggest guns available before it gets any closer to the bottom. Don't worry—you'll probably be home in a few hours." He turned on his heels and disappeared down the hall.

But at 2:00 AM the nurse called Holmes and me out of the cubicle. "Your son is not responding as well as he should be. You'll have to admit him to the hospital. If you'll just go down the hall to Admitting and sign the papers, we'll get him upstairs to a room."

My spirits fell like the rain pelting the window beside me. Swallowing a huge lump in my throat, I thought about the yellow Snoopy lunch box Justin had picked out, the new jeans, and the red-plaid shirt already laid out on his bunk bed for his first big day of school. "Holmes, there's no way he'll be well enough to start school!"

"I think we have a lot more to worry about than school," he bristled. After we got our son all settled in his fifth-floor room, Holmes sent me home to stay with our other children, Alison and Chris, while he kept vigil at Justin's bedside. I just *knew* he would be better in the morning.

But when I walked in at 8:00 AM, Justin was white-faced, an oxygen tube in his nose. The muscles in his neck and chest strained as he fought for air. Every breath sounded like a rib-rattling staccato.

In spite of other treatments, his condition worsened throughout the day. On his afternoon rounds, Dr. Spencer examined him again, shook his head, and took us out in the hall.

"Something inside his body has got to rally. I've done everything I know to do," he told us.

Stunned, I couldn't believe what I had just heard. My heart raced. The rising anxiety cracked the thin veneer of calm I had tried so hard to maintain.

"Why don't you go home for a while?" Holmes said.

"But I can't leave now."

"You've got to nurse Alison and reassure Chris. They haven't seen you for hours. Besides, you aren't much help unless you pull yourself together. You're only making him nervous," my husband said.

I hated to leave, but I knew he was right. In a dazed fog, I rode the elevator down and walked out the front door of the hospital. A loud clap of thunder startled me. A slap of cold rain stung my face. I searched up and down the rows of parked cars, but could not find our station wagon anywhere. Finally, soaked and shivering, I dashed back into the hospital to wait for the storm to let up. Huddling next to the door, I noticed the sign: Chapel.

Reluctantly I slipped into the empty chapel and was drawn to the large white Bible at the front, open to Psalm 42:

> Why are you downcast, O my soul?
> Why so disturbed within me?
> Put your hope in God, for I will yet praise him,
> 　　my Savior and my God.

Finally, in the quiet I prayed, "Lord, I have put my hope in the doctor, the medicine, in Holmes, and in myself to save Justin. That's why I'm in so much despair and fear. I've trusted You in some areas of my life, but I've clung to my kids, trying to keep them safe myself. I even dedicated them in a church service, but I never really entrusted them totally to Your care. I'm like the disciples who in the midst of a fierce storm, cried out to Jesus, 'Master, Master, we are perishing!'"

And a quiet inner voice said to me as He had said to the disciples, *Cheri, where is your faith? Peace…be still.*

Lightning caused the chapel lights to flicker off and on, and thunder boomed outside, turning my thoughts again to God.

The Creator of the whole universe was in complete command of the thunderstorm outside, yet I couldn't trust Him with my son's life. In not releasing him to God's care, I was thwarting the very power that could help him.

Hope in Me, I felt Him say. *Trust his life to Me totally.*

I bowed my head and this time said, "Father, forgive me for not trusting him to Your care sooner. I forgot that he was Your child first and that You made him. I give him to You, whatever happens."

As I walked outside, something warm began to melt away that icy fear that had gripped me. The torrent of rain had turned to a drizzle. After searching several rows in the parking lot, I found our car.

I drove up the hill to get on the expressway. When I slowed at the Yield sign, I looked up and was struck by a tiny sliver of terrifically bright sunshine that broke through the angry, black clouds.

At that moment a huge weight lifted inside me, and a feeling of peace unlike I had ever experienced swept through me. Justin was safe and cared for. In some inexplicable way I knew it, and knew I could trust God with our precious firstborn son.

I spent a happy, unhurried hour with Chris and Alison in our favorite yellow rocking chair at home, munching cheese and crackers and reading Richard Scarry books to them.

An hour and a half later I returned to the hospital and walked into our son's room. He was sitting up in bed, coloring a picture, and chatting with his grandparents who had just arrived from East Texas. A smile lit up his rosy face as he asked, "Mom, when can I go home and see Chris and Alison and puppy?"

Although Justin still battled asthma in the years to come, his treatment never required hospitalization again. When I packed his Snoopy lunch box on his first day of school, I sent him off with a deep sense of peace. I would not be there to protect him.

But I knew the One who would.

Healing took place not only in our son that day, but also in me because my focus changed from the afflicting problem to God. As I saw Him anew as the all-powerful, almighty Lord for whom nothing is too difficult, as I experienced His love in the midst of our crisis, the tight grip that fear had over me was broken. Just as God reached inside Justin's body to restore his breathing and oxygen level, He reached deep inside me to my heart and emotions to restore trust. From that point on, when the asthma attacks came, over and over God's perfect love cast out fear.

As the years passed, our son still had asthma but grew stronger each year. He was a varsity tennis player for his high school, and in his twenties became a long-distance runner for whom marathons are a breeze—even completing rugged 50-mile trail runs. God has surprises around the bend as we trust Him!

* Adapted from *Fearless: Building a Faith That Overcomes Your Fear* by Cheri Fuller (Revell, 2003).

You can never pray too long or too much. In order to help her autistic son, Cori knew she would have to do both.

☙ *Shattered Dreams* ❧

BY CORI SMELKER, SAN ANTONIO, TEXAS

"Mrs. Smelker, based on my examination, along with the pediatric reports and test results, Carson has all the classic symptoms of autism."

I knew the doctor was right, but Carson is my baby, the last of five children. My heart sank as I realized she had voiced my worst fear. I had a child with "special needs." My heart was shattered as my dream for five "normal" children was unrealized.

"Perhaps he's just a late bloomer. After all, he's my fifth child, the fourth in three years. Maybe he's not getting the attention he needs. Is that right, Lord?" I questioned the diagnosis, even though I knew the symptoms were obvious.

When Carson turned ten months of age, his behavior changed drastically. He stopped interacting with his siblings and made minimal eye contact with other people.

The most telling moment came in December 2000. While having lunch with a dear friend, Aleta, and four of my children, including Carson, she noticed my son sitting completely still in his high chair. He was completely oblivious to everything around him, except the Christmas decorations dangling from the ceiling. "Cori, you need to take him to a specialist. This is just not normal." Looking at my son, I knew she was right.

I visited several doctors and received several opinions, but none conclusive: "He could be a late bloomer," or "All children develop at different rates." So we decided to wait. Carson was only a year old.

We waited six months. At 18 months of age, I returned to the doctor with my son. I explained how he had to watch the same video repeatedly, how he played with only one toy, and how the ceiling fan captivated him. I told him how Carson would lean against the washer for hours at a time, feeling the vibrations, how he sucked on his clothing until it was filled with holes.

"I think it's time we send him to the MIND Clinic (Michigan Institute for Neurological Disorders)." Our doctor readied the necessary paperwork, and we made an appointment with the recommended specialist.

After a battery of tests, observations, and MRIs, we heard the dreaded word *autism*.

"Autism, Lord? Why? This is every parent's nightmare, certainly mine." I explained the situation to Him, as if He didn't understand my predicament. "Autism means a child who's locked away in a prison of his own making, a child whose compulsions are so bad he can fly into a rage if his world is disturbed. Autism is a child who conceivably can't give or return affection.

"Carson's not like that." I raised my voice, wanting to yell. "My son is affectionate." In reality, Carson was prone to biting anyone who got in his way. He would "drift away" as he retreated into his own mental world. He felt safe there.

Carson was two and a half years old when we received another neurology report. Our son was ready to attend preprimary intervention classes with teachers trained to work specifically with autistic children. My husband and I read voraciously about autism, trying to figure out how to serve our son's needs.

Terry and I prayed constantly, and our church family supported us with prayer as well. "Father, we know You can heal our precious little boy. Will You?"

A few days later, my husband and I visited a different church. They were hosting a speaker from South Africa. I had heard him before, and his ministry had impacted me in the past.

"Teach Us to Pray" was the title of his message that night. I will never forget it. During ministry time he spoke with Terry and me. "One of your children is a concern for you, and you worry about him. It's okay. God will take care of it all. He will take care of it. Your child is His, and He will take care of him. That's God's promise to you."

I wasn't sure whether to laugh or cry. I think I probably did a little of both. This man didn't know us, knew nothing about our family, yet he spoke of our situation. He didn't know the diagnosis we had received days earlier. This wasn't even our church.

From that night forward, Carson was significantly different. At two and a half, our son only had a one-word vocabulary, but by Christmas, three days later, his vocabulary had increased to more than 20 words. He also developed a sudden interest in multiple toys, and was now playing with them appropriately. If he drifted into "dream world," we could easily pull him out of it.

Recently our family relocated from Commerce, Michigan, to San Antonio, Texas. We wanted to make sure Carson got the same intervention in Texas that he had received in Michigan, so we enrolled him in a class for children with developmental delays. Based on the reports from the Michigan school district, our son qualified for the program.

One morning after I had dropped Carson off at school, the phone rang and I answered it.

"Mrs. Smelker, this is Carson's teacher. I want to ask for your permission to have him retested, because the child we're dealing with here is not the same child described in his case files."

"Why, what's wrong?" I squeezed the phone cord, twisting it in my fingers.

"That's just it. There's nothing wrong. He's doing so well, we really don't think he fits the same profile anymore."

One month later, Terry and I met with the teacher, the speech therapist, the psychologist, and the physical therapist.

"Mr. and Mrs. Smelker, based on our examinations, we are pleased to announce that there are no signs of autism in Carson. He's a perfectly normal, highly intelligent boy, performing one to two years above his age group. We can't include him in this program any longer and recommend you enroll him in a regular preschool."

I'm not sure how or why God chose to heal our son, but when I look into Carson's eyes, I see the healing power of Jesus. I am so thankful He chose to answer this mother's prayers.

> Although praying for our children takes precedence over all other prayers in a mom's life, we sometimes need to pray for ourselves, just so we can be around to keep praying.

～ The Gift of Life ～

BY NANCY B. GIBBS, CORDELE, GEORGIA

God blessed me with twin sons over 31 years ago. They were perfect babies and have grown into fine young men. For a few days after they were born, I was very sick. I had lost a great deal of blood, and it was touch-and-go for a while. While other women were being admitted to the hospital, having babies, and going home, I was unable to even stand up. Since I had a very high temperature, I was not permitted to hold or even see my new infant sons.

The third day after the delivery, the doctors discovered my blood count was dangerously low. A nurse came in to draw blood and panicked. My veins had apparently started to collapse. The doctor quietly slipped into my room and sat down in the chair beside me.

"Without blood, Nancy, you may not make it through the night," he said candidly. "With blood transfusions, you may have a chance."

The doctor continued. "But there is something else you must do. For every pint of blood you receive, the hospital needs two pints of donated blood in return." They had no idea how much blood it would take to make me well. Apparently this was their way of keeping the blood supply available for other people who needed the gift of life.

"You wouldn't believe how many people are downstairs giving blood for you, honey," my daddy whispered, as he washed my forehead with a cool cloth. "I know you're going to be fine. There are so many people pulling for you."

My family had been petitioning for blood. Many people volunteered to make a donation in my behalf. They told their friends about my need, and within a few hours, more than enough blood had been obtained.

Daddy turned his head away to wipe tears from his eyes. I was too weak to even speak. Even though I couldn't respond verbally, my heart was filled with hope and gratitude for the ones who cared so much.

Lord, please make me well so I can thank these life-savers personally.

Suddenly, even though I continued to feel horrible, the fear I had previously felt disappeared. I knew if God had entrusted me with two healthy baby boys, He would allow me to stay around to raise them. I realized that my infirmity was a small price to pay for the love I was to receive for many years to come.

After a transfusion of several pints of blood, I began feeling better. My energy level increased and, after a couple more days, I was able to go home to raise my tiny sons.

We have always been very close, and today—more than 30 years later—I remain grateful that God answered my prayer that day. I am also grateful to the people who gave, whether they gave blood themselves or petitioned for blood on my behalf. These people may have saved my life.

My doctors weren't sure that I would make it through the night some 31 years ago, but thankfully, the Great Physician had different plans for me. He blessed me with the opportunity to enjoy many hugs and kisses while my sons were growing up. He also sent a wonderful daughter my way five years later.

Today I have three precious granddaughters to hold and love. When I gaze into their tiny eyes, I'm thankful that God gave me the chance to raise my children and then to know the joy of being a grandparent. With a love like His given from above, we have absolutely nothing to fear, regardless of the difficulties that stand before us.

The gift of life comes to us in various ways. The blood transfusions saved my life, and my family made my life worth living. God worked the miracle that made it all happen, not because I had done anything to deserve it, but simply because He loves me so much.

Sometimes medical doctors have no idea how an injured child can recover so quickly. But a praying mom knows the answer.

∽ *The Dreaded Piggyback Ride* ∾

BY SHAREN WATSON, SPRING, TEXAS

"Okay, that's it. No more procrastination!" I said aloud, scolding myself for browsing away most of the morning at the mall.

I turned the key in the ignition, firing up the engine of my little Nissan wagon. Pulling out of the parking lot, I was determined to accomplish my goals for the day: finding, buying, and preparing this Sunday's lesson for a classroom full of energetic preschool children. Course firmly set and mind clearly focused on the task ahead, I cruised down the highway toward the only Christian bookstore in town.

"Lord, You know exactly what's needed to teach Your sweet children. Will You please help me choose the right materials that will capture their attention and lead their little hearts toward You? Thank You so much. Amen."

My exit was just ahead.

While signaling to change lanes, I noticed perspiration building on my hands, so I adjusted my grip on the steering wheel to keep them from slipping. I felt tension beginning to make its way through my upper back, spreading into my neck, and an uneasy sense of apprehension permeated my mind.

"What's wrong with me?" I sat up taller, concentrating on breathing evenly to combat the increasing anxiety.

My ramp was just ahead, and I signaled my intent to exit. I was determined to complete my errand, but a deeper determination to promptly find my way home prevailed. So I turned off the blinker and continued down the highway.

Disappointed with my lack of productivity, I tossed my purse and keys down next to me as I sank into the couch. I still couldn't shake the tension pulling through my shoulders and neck, and my pulse was racing. I stood to my feet, stretched, took a deep breath, and walked into the kitchen to look for some Advil.

The phone, set on its highest volume, startled me with an unexpected ring, completely throwing off my concentration. The open bottle of Advil in my hand went flying. Caplets tumbled everywhere, scattering all over the kitchen floor. Any expectation of slowing my rapid pulse was beyond hopeless.

"H-h-hello…speaking…is she okay? I will be right there."

A jolt of adrenaline shot through me, instantaneously replacing every trace of tension and anxiety. Grabbing my things, I rushed out to the car.

"She has a large bump on the back of her head," explained the school secretary. "We've been holding ice on it to keep the swelling down, but it's very painful to the touch."

I looked down at my ten-year-old daughter weeping quietly in my arms. "How did this happen?"

After hearing the secretary's brief explanation, I picked up my little girl and carried her to the car. As I buckled her into the passenger seat, I tried to remember the various symptoms of severe head injury and concussion.

"Mommy…mama, water," my little girl cried.

I handed her my water bottle, but she pushed it away.

"Mama, my ears!"

Trying to concentrate on driving, I glanced at her momentarily, but long enough to see her cheek was smudged with blood. Her ears were draining and her nose was bleeding. I reached for the only thing I could find to clean her up: my sweater.

Pulling into the pediatrician's parking lot, I whisked my daughter out of the passenger seat and rushed in. As soon as the receptionist saw my daughter, she hurried us into the examination room. We had barely made it to the table, and the nurse was scrambling for a sick pan.

Leaving me momentarily to tend to my daughter, she went in search of the doctor.

"Tell me what happened, Sharen." The doctor needed every ounce of information I could provide.

"I wasn't there when she fell, but I can tell you what I was told by the school secretary." I took hold of my listless daughter's hand. She seemed to be drifting in and out of consciousness.

"Go on." She waited for the details while calmly continuing her examination.

"From what I understand, a friend was carrying her on his back."

"Oh…the dreaded piggyback ride, huh?" The doctor nodded and smiled, putting me temporarily at ease.

"Yes, and well, evidently she let go to be put down, and her friend did not release her legs, and she…" I cringed at the thought of what had happened, "she fell backwards, hitting her head on the blacktop."

"Shawna, I want you to stay awake. Do you hear me, sweetheart? I am going to take you for a short ride in my car, okay?" Dr. Bhogal gently nudged my daughter and signaled her nurses to prepare my daughter for transport.

"Sharen, do I have your permission to take your daughter in my vehicle to the hospital?"

I nodded.

"You can follow me over," she said, making sure I was fully aware of her request.

I nodded again. "Okay."

Keeping my sights on the yellow Jaguar was easy, but the challenge was keeping an even closer eye on my daughter's movements. I could see the doctor trying to keep Shawna engaged in conversation, and under normal circumstances I would have seen my daughter's hands moving simultaneously with each animated word. But through the glare of the windshield, I couldn't make out any movement at all.

"Oh Father, please help my baby girl." I couldn't think of any more to say.

When we arrived at the hospital, they were ready for her. While I filled out all the necessary forms, the doctor wheeled Shawna to the CAT scan room.

"We need her results, stat," I heard her say, as she disappeared down the hall.

The doctor's suspicions were confirmed. Shawna had sustained a severe concussion and fractured skull. She was admitted to the hospital for continuing observation.

And we waited.

"Oh Lord," I prayed, while gently smoothing my daughter's hair from her face, "please, heal my baby girl."

Repeating the same prayer over and over again, I never looked away from my beloved sleeping child. And when exhaustion at last closed my eyes, God's eyes never left her.

Throughout the night, nurses kept track of her vitals, and a neurosurgeon came to check on her progress. Through it all, Shawna slept peacefully.

The first signs of daylight streamed through the cracks of the mini blinds, and Shawna stirred. I opened my eyes slowly to adjust to the morning light. I had fallen asleep with my head leaning on the hospital bed rail, using part of my daughter's blanket to soften my makeshift pillow.

"Mommy, I'm hungry."

"Hungry? Let's see if we can get a nurse to take care of that." I reached immediately for the call button.

When the nurse came in, Shawna was attempting to sit up, so we adjusted the bed and intravenous tubes to accommodate her.

"How are you feeling this morning, Shawna?" the nurse asked, as she proceeded to check my daughter's blood pressure.

"Good, but I'm hungry. Do you have any pancakes?"

The nurse looked at me and smiled. "I'll see what I can do."

Later that morning, the children's pastor from our church came to visit. When he arrived, the neurologist was checking on Shawna's progress...in the playroom! Aside from being hungry, she was tired of being bedridden, and when she heard there was a toy room, she had no time to waste propped up on pillows. So with the help of the nurse, we rigged her IV up to wheels, and she was off. Pastor Pete had difficulty keeping up with her to pray, and when he did get her to settle down, he could barely get a word in. She was chattering away with hand gestures to rival sign language.

The neurologist was stunned. He told me he had rarely seen a child with her extent of injury recuperate so rapidly. He tested her verbal skills and physical coordination. Everything was normal, so he recommended my daughter's release from the hospital after a few more hours of observation and a couple of meals. The only directions he specified were limits on physical activity, two weeks' absence from school to recuperate, and a couple of follow-up visits with her pediatrician. He left me with directions to care for her swelling, pain medication (if necessary), and a list of warning symptoms to watch for.

Two weeks later she was back in school.

Twelve years have passed since that time. Shawna graduated from college this year and is engaged to be married. Only one small reminder of her skull fracture remains with her today: a minuscule bald spot on her scalp.

I thanked the Lord then, and I continue to thank Him now, for saving my daughter from a life-threatening injury and for the signals of urgency driving me home.

When Mary Ann prayed for her daughter to be healed, it took a powerful amount of faith. Gina was diagnosed with a fatal lymph-gland disorder, but miracles can and do happen every day. Mary Ann knew that and believed it.

⌐: *The Power of Faith* :~

BY MARY ANN L. DIORIO, PH.D., MILLVILLE, NEW JERSEY

"She looks pale," the pediatrician said as he examined my two-month-old daughter. "I want to run some blood work on her."

My heart lurched at the doctor's words. *What could be wrong?* Our second daughter had had a potentially dangerous delivery, with a double-knotted umbilical cord wrapped twice around her neck. By God's grace, the obstetrician had quickly averted what could have been a tragic situation.

Now this! "Lord," I cried out, "I don't know what's happening, but whatever it is, I will trust in You."

When I told my husband about the doctor's diagnosis, he called a friend of ours who was a minister. The three of us joined hands around our daughter Gina and prayed for her healing. Then we waited for the test results.

One test indicated intestinal bleeding. Ruling out the most common possible causes, our pediatrician sent us to St. Christopher's Children's Hospital in Philadelphia for further tests.

One of the tests required overnight fasting. When I heard the instructions, my heart sank. "Lord, You know Gina nurses every two hours. Hearing my baby scream in hunger all night is more than I can bear. Please help us!"

As my maternal heart fought fear and worry, I chose again to trust in God. To my indescribable joy, for the first time in her young life, Gina slept through the night. Not only did she sleep through the night, but she also slept through the hour-long ride to the hospital and through the entire medical procedure. When she finally awoke, it was nine o'clock in the morning. I had a very hungry baby on my hands!

After the tests and examinations, we were told Gina had an incurable lymph-gland disorder. While the news rocked our souls, it did not rock our spirits. We continued to cling to God's promise of healing and prayed for our dear daughter.

One afternoon shortly after the hospital visit, Gina was sleeping in her cradle in the family room. Sitting beside her, I felt the need to turn on the television to the 700 Club. As I tuned in, Dr. Pat Robertson was praying. The very next words out of his mouth were, "There's a baby in the TV audience with a lymph-gland disorder, and God is healing her right now."

Like an eagle taking wing, I flew out of my chair shouting, "That's my Gina! That's my Gina!" As I raised my hands in worship and praise, I thanked the Lord for His message of hope.

Following this miraculous event, I took Gina back to the pediatrician. He could find no signs of bleeding, and her blood count had returned to normal.

Today our Gina is a beautiful 27-year-old young woman who is serving the Lord with all her heart, soul, strength, and mind. She is a living testimony not only of God's power to heal, but also of His great desire to do so. May He be praised forevermore.

6
Trying Times

HAVE YOU EVER THOUGHT about the armor of God? There are no back parts to it. True! But let's think about it for a minute. We have the helmet of salvation, the breastplate of righteousness, the belt of truth. Then there are the weapons: the shield of faith and the sword of the Spirit. None of that offers covering from the back, though.

But have you ever taught a young child how to write or how to cut with scissors? His hand is in yours. You are in back of him, yet you are leading and guiding him through the process. The same thing happens with God.

You have a promise from your Lord that He will lead and guide you through trying times. Take Him at His Word. If God can speak the world into existence and make His Word become flesh, He can get you through this difficult situation, too. Do not be afraid. Remember, He's got your back.

❦❦❦

For I am the LORD, your God, who takes hold of your right hand
and says to you, Do not fear; I will help you.

ISAIAH 41:13

We teach our children to pray and to believe in the power of prayer. Sometimes moms need a child's belief to show them God's faithful answer.

⌇ *Dancing in Red Velvet* ⌇

BY EILEEN KEY, SAN ANTONIO, TEXAS

I stood in my new home surrounded by boxes, wondering what to unpack first. My husband's new job had taken us to a small town in the Rio Grande Valley of Texas. We now had a larger home, yet I still wondered where everything would fit. Daunted by the task at hand, I perched on the arm of the sofa, thankful for the cool air cranked out by the air conditioner. May 1, 1985, had dawned sunny and humid—typical for Donna, Texas.

My five-year-old daughter, Sarah, bounced into the room. My reverie interrupted, I glanced her way. She was wearing her long, red-velvet Christmas dress.

"Don't I look pretty?" She pirouetted and pranced before me. "Don't I, Mommy?"

"You're gorgeous." I took her hand and twirled her around. "Where are you going so dressed up?"

"I'm going outside to meet my new friend." Sarah smiled and patted the folds of her dress. She rubbed the smooth velvet texture first one way, then another to make designs.

"What new friend?" My voice held a note of anxiety. Last time I had checked, our new neighborhood was as still as the muggy air.

"Mommy, you said Jesus would send me a friend when we moved here, so I want to look pretty when I meet her. Do you think she'll like my dress?" An upturned face smiled expectantly. "I can't wait to dance and play with my new friend."

How did I tackle this?

To encourage Sarah before our move, I had talked of meeting friends and visiting different places. We had prayed together often about our new home, asking the Lord to bless us as we changed locations.

Before I waxed poetic about God's timing, my daughter bounded out the French doors, skipped to the chain-link fence, and pressed her face to the crisscrossed metal.

I watched. She stood and waited.

A prick of sorrow touched me. *Why can't I have an expectant heart like Sarah's, Lord? I'm new in the neighborhood, too.*

I turned back to work with a deep sigh, worried about my daughter's disappointment, and whispered a prayer for her. I unpacked two boxes and then peeked outside. I almost fainted. A little girl with long, black pigtails stood beside the fence. She and Sarah talked and giggled, their fingers intertwined in the mesh.

I stepped onto the patio, and Sarah caught sight of me. "Hi, Mommy. This is Erica, and she's five like me. She lives next door. She wants to play. Is that okay?" The girls gazed at me, melting my insides as only five-year-olds can.

I nodded. A smile burst in my heart. Sarah believed in what she had been told and acted on it. Sarah had expected and prayed for a friend, and God had answered her prayer.

I walked indoors.

"Lord, I need a new friend, too," I whispered, searching through the scattered boxes. "Now where is that box with my red-velvet Christmas dress?"

Not only are our prayers for our children's spiritual growth important, so also are our prayers for them for a great education and a love of learning. Through Vicki's strong faith in prayer, she found out just how well it works.

◡ *My Son, Humpty Dumpty* ◡

BY VICKI CARUANA, COLORADO SPRINGS, COLORADO

"Lord, please restore Charles's love for learning, no matter who his teacher is or what program he's in." This became my nightly prayer.

Moving mountains to help my students would not be too big a task. My desire as a teacher has always been to encourage and educate kids to strive for excellence. Imagine how discouraging it was to realize that not all teachers think like this. What was even more discouraging was that this lack of desire affected my own child.

Charles, our youngest son, is very bright. As a teacher I knew the importance of placing him in a program that would challenge him and satisfy his thirst for knowledge. At the time it seemed like an excellent plan, but it turned out to be a plan that didn't work.

Little by little, the demands of this accelerated program broke my son's will to learn. I just didn't understand the change. How could my bright and beautiful child now hate school and despise learning? I talked to him and to his teachers. No matter what I did or said, he continued to spiral downward into depression.

"Dear Lord," I prayed, "please soften the hearts of his teachers toward him so they can encourage him. Please let my words reach him and help him to regain his love of learning. Please help deliver him from this trial."

I knew that if he could just get through this, he would be a stronger and more resilient person. But things just got worse and worse.

In desperation I repeated my nightly prayer: "Lord, please restore Charles's love for learning, no matter who his teacher is or what program he's in," with the added line of, "and please make it soon!"

Sometimes God answers our prayers in the most unusual ways. The answer doesn't always look like you expect it to. In fact, sometimes it doesn't look like an answer at all.

What happened at recess the next day can only be described as foolishness. When two sixth-grade boys begin a game of pushing, what else do you expect to happen? Charles fell backward onto the concrete, putting out his right hand to break his fall. He not only dislocated his wrist, but broke it in five places! He literally fell to pieces!

I went to school to let them know my son's new limitations and asked for their help so Charles would not fall behind during the last six weeks of school. They offered no options, no strategies, and no encouragement. "I guess he'll have a hard time keeping up" was the best they had to offer. It broke my heart to see such apathy. I could not and would not let my son stay in this environment.

We pulled our son out of school for the remainder of the year and I homeschooled him. It was amazing how he began to thrive. He more than made up the missed work, he finished ahead of schedule. I watched as slowly but surely his lost love for learning returned. The fire was reignited, and a smile spread across his precious face each and every morning. Amazing!

When he went back to school the next year, we made some changes. We took him out of the advanced program and placed him back in the regular classroom environment. He thrived! He loved his teachers and his classes. He made more friends than he had any other year. The bundle of anxiety and dread that was my son now excels in his studies and cannot wait to go to school each day.

God answered a mother's prayer. Charles again loves to learn. The trauma of a shattered wrist is not exactly how I would have done it, but God knows what is best for each of us. He knows what will make the difference. The X-rays my son so proudly shows to his friends aren't just evidence of his trauma, but also of his healing. God put all the pieces back together again, and they are working just fine!

> Raising a child as a single parent is a difficult process. Prayer can sometimes be the only anchor holding everything together.

⌁ *When the Only Language I Have Is My Tears* ⌁

BY KARI WEST, PLEASANTON, CALIFORNIA

The day I moved into single parenting, I was weighed down with more than cardboard boxes. *Whose pain do I deal with first?* I wondered. I thought back to three months earlier, only 14 days before Christmas, when I had sorted the mail after work: a stack of season's greetings in one hand, a divorce summons in the other. With tears coursing down my cheeks, I had told my 12-year-old daughter, "Melanie, this was never my dream for you."

"But you promised, Mom, that you and Dad would never get a divorce. You said you could always talk things out!" she screamed. "I hate you! I don't want to be anything like you. I don't want to talk like you, dress like you, act like you, or look like you, because Daddy left you!"

Out of words and bereft of answers, I sobbed in a silent place beyond words, recalling the day I stood at an altar vowing love for a lifetime, unwanted divorce never entering my mind. I had trusted in a God who could turn evil into good ever since accepting Jesus into my heart as a young girl. Now I wondered how He would do it this time.

As the months wore on, I often thought about giving up. Overwhelmed by the stunning discovery of multiple affairs going back years and the myriad of legal and day-to-day tasks, I soon saw that the parenting rules I had relied on no longer worked. It seemed my ex-husband continually tried to throw me off balance.

"At Daddy's place I don't have to clean my room or dig dandelions," Melanie often snarled. "And why don't you have money for pizza? Daddy buys it for me."

Each day raced further out of control. I felt my child becoming an enemy in my camp as her father used information from her to rearrange my work plans on weekends when she was scheduled to stay with him. Extravagant gifts filled her bedroom: 50-dollar perfume, a leather jacket, a dozen roses, a TV and stereo system—luxuries my ex-husband had never condoned spoiling our daughter with before the divorce.

Soon behavior problems escalated in school as her grades plummeted. *I have lost her*, I thought. Of course there were those who advised, "Put her in a foster home." "Give Melanie to her dad." But regardless of those comments and the chaos of being a single, working mom, I could not imagine walking away. Instead I chose a yearly verse, reading 1 Peter 5:10 each morning before work and asking God to make me "strong, firm, and steadfast."

Several months later I ran into a business acquaintance with whom I had once worked. "If your daughter makes it," he said, "it will be with you. You're the best parent for the job."

That night at the foot of an empty bed, with sleep evading me as the tapes in my brain replayed "should do this" and "could do that," I knelt and gave God all I had left: my life, my health, my job, my future, my daughter. I prayed for truth and pleaded for courage to commit for the long haul and boldly live out what I believe.

Within days my commitment was tested. I refused to play the popularity game. "I can't compete with 'Popcorn Daddy' by giving you everything you want," I told Melanie. "All I can give you is what I think you need: a love that knows how to say no, the stability of a home you can call your own, consistency—whether you think I am old-fashioned or a meany—and values like taking responsibility and believing that being a good person is more important than feeling good."

Keeping my equilibrium was hard. It took days to return to normal living after Melanie came back from Wednesday-night outings with her dad and every other weekend at his place. One night, friends had to scrape me off the ceiling with a spatula. "I want to come home, Mom. Can you pick me up?" she asked, calling from a bar during one visitation.

My daughter was often arrogant, authoritarian, and verbally abusive, like on that first Mother's Day after dining in a fancy restaurant with her dad and his girlfriend. "She's so pretty," Melanie told me. "She'd make a much better mother than you."

Over time I realized that divorce ends a marriage, but it does not terminate a family. The resistance I experienced from my daughter started making sense: Her history and past family traditions had crumbled. Nothing stayed the same. Even birthdays and holidays were negotiated. She felt torn between being loyal to me and choosing her dad, who was and always had been her idol. She was lashing out at me because she felt unsure of his commitment to her. She knew, whatever she said and did, that she could count on my love—even though she dare not admit it.

Caught in this puzzling dilemma that I could not change or fix, I kept telling my daughter, "I love you, and I am being the best parent I can be." When I no longer had energy to argue over homework, I allowed her to fail high-school algebra the first time through. And when she returned from a sixteenth-birthday trip with her dad and said, "I am going on a blind date Friday, like it or not," I arrived at a turning point.

Melanie already knew the parameters around her dating: Mom meets the boy and whoever is driving. This time she vehemently objected, saying her dad told her she needed to be in a serious relationship by the time she was 18. Since he had joint custody, he had given her permission. Although I couldn't rush the settling of her undulating emotions nor hold back the fear that stormed my heart, I refused to be held hostage any longer in my own home.

I pulled out her suitcase and said, "Then your dad can have total responsibility raising you. I won't watch you destroy yourself and pick up the pieces afterward." Her door slammed. I trembled. She stayed.

Now there is little my daughter and I cannot talk about. She finally saw that home and family are not about a big house and perfect people but about listening ears, open hearts, and warm hugs. I think she caught on that, whatever happens, her mom is her biggest fan.

Not long ago Melanie and I were driving to the mall, talking about finally becoming friends and reminiscing about all those years she hated me. "Mom, don't you get it? You were the rock. You never moved," she said. "While I love Dad a lot, I couldn't count on him. Sure, I could do anything I wanted at his house. But he never kept his word. I never knew where he stood."

Tears filled my eyes. I remembered the many times I had retreated to the sanctuary of my bedroom, out of answers and out of strength. I had lifted my weary arms to the sky, imagining my daughter lying across my open palms, and prayed, *"Lord, You've got a big problem. I don't know what to do anymore about Melanie. I am so tired and so scared. She's Yours; I give her back to You."*

In those desperate moments, I was leaning on strength greater than I knew and on a love broader than I could imagine. Only with hindsight do I really see with the eyes of my heart what was there all along and always will be: an unchangeable God, who bottles my tears and is my immovable Rock; Jesus, who intercedes for me and is the one and only Lover who will never leave; the Holy Spirit, who leads me into truth and understands all the words when the only language I have is my tears.

Sometimes no matter what we do or say, our children decide to do "their own thing." Turning their entire life over to the Lord in prayer might be the only course of action to take.

⌁ The Power of Prayer ⌁

BY SUSAN PEABODY, BERKELEY, CALIFORNIA

I have believed in God most of my life, but until a few years ago I had no faith in prayer. One day all of that changed.

My son, Karl, was 12 years old when his father died. I tried to comfort him, but he just got angry and barricaded himself in his bedroom.

"I don't care," he said.

But I could hear him crying on the other side of the door.

At the age of 14, he entered high school. Right from the start he had difficulty adjusting. When his first report card came, it indicated he was failing all of his classes because of poor attendance.

I talked for long hours to Karl about this. I went to endless parent-teacher meetings at the high school. I sent him to counseling. I went to counseling with him. I tried punishing him, even begging. Nothing worked.

Every day I dropped him off at the high school entrance on my way to work, and after I drove away, he crossed the street and hung out in the park with the other dropouts.

The low point for me came the day I received Karl's report card and a letter from the school's Talented and Gifted Program. The report card indicated that Karl had been absent most of the semester, received six failing grades, and was now a full year behind his classmates. The letter said, "Your son was given an IQ test, and it indicates that he has above-average intelligence. Please call our office to discuss his future. We are convinced that he will do well in our college-bound program. He is exceptionally bright."

This was the last straw for me. I couldn't get Karl to go to school, much less to a program asking for extra effort. I felt so powerless and unable to cope that I simply started crying. After what seemed like hours, I dried my tears.

For the first time since I was a child, I began to really pray. "God, please take my son into Your loving arms and dry his tears. Please be the father that Karl needs. God, I know Karl has great potential. Please help him to achieve what he is capable of accomplishing."

When I finished praying, I was rewarded with a sense of peace I hadn't known in years. That night I slept like a baby, fully convinced that everything was going to be all right. From that point on, I stopped all my efforts to make Karl go to school. I turned the whole situation over to God, and I waited.

A few weeks later the phone rang while I was sitting at my desk at work. A man with a deep voice asked for Karl's mother.

"That's me," I replied. "What can I do for you?"

"I am Karl's school counselor," the man replied. "I want to talk to you about your son's absences."

"Oh," I said. "I'm glad to hear from you, but I want you to know that I've already tried everything to get Karl to go to school. Now it is up to the Lord."

With these words I began crying and pouring out my heart to this stranger on the phone. "I love my son," I said. "I only want what is best for him. I can't make him do something he refuses to do. God knows I have tried. So I am going to pray for him and love him, no matter what he decides to do with his life. That's all I can do for now."

When I was finished, there was silence on the other end of the line. Solemnly the man finally said, "Thank you for your time, Mrs. Peabody. I will stay in touch."

Karl's next report card showed a marked improvement in his attendance and grades. I was ecstatic. The following semester Karl was on the honor roll. I couldn't believe the change I had prayed for was actually happening.

For the next two years, Karl continued to work hard. He went to summer school and evening classes at the local adult school to make up the classes he had failed. He was determined to graduate with his class.

Halfway through Karl's last semester in high school, he asked me to go to Parents' Night. He squired me around from classroom to classroom introducing me to his teachers. They all told me how happy they were about Karl's improvement.

Before we went home that night, Karl escorted me to a patio adjacent to the school gym. It was a beautiful night. The moon was full and the stars were bright. Karl and I sat down on a wooden bench, just enjoying the moment.

We were both silent for a while, and Karl turned to me with a smile on his face. He hesitated for a second, then softly said, "Mom, you've never asked me why I went back to school. Don't you want to know?"

"Sure I do," I replied. "I've just been so happy about the change in you that I didn't want to question it."

"Well," he said, "I'd like to tell you. A while back, I decided to play a joke on you. I called you at work and pretended to be a school counselor. For some reason, you didn't recognize my voice and you shared with me your innermost feelings about the problems I was having. What you said saddened me and made me ashamed. Suddenly I knew deep in my heart that I had to do something to make things right. From that moment on, I resolved to do better—for myself and for you."

I couldn't speak. I was amazed. Then I gave Karl a hug and silently thanked the Lord for answering my prayer in such an inventive way. I praised God for also transforming me in the process. Without prayer, my spiritual life was dead. The Lord showed me that I could make a U-turn back to communicating with Him. Now my spirit soars with each and every prayer I send to heaven.

And Karl? He graduated with honors from Berkeley High School in 1989. He went on to the University of California at Berkeley, and received his degree in 1993. He finished his education with an MBA from Dominican College San Rafael in 1995. And I still pray for him.

Praying for our child to find that "someone special" is a major concern of moms. Joan prayed for her son, Lane. Although it took a couple of tries, she was not sorry at the outcome.

↙ Ruth and Naomi—an Answered Prayer ↝

BY JOAN CLAYTON, PORTALES, NEW MEXICO

I had been praying for my son Lane's mate since the day he was born. He and his girlfriend were at "outs" again. It seemed to me they disagreed about anything and everything. So when I heard about their engagement, I was a little apprehensive. I liked her well enough, but wondered if she were the right one for Lane.

Now that they were engaged, my daily prayer became, "Lord, if this isn't the girl for Lane, please send the right one."

During my prayer one night, I had a vision. With closed eyes I saw two girls. No mistake about it: the girl on the left was Lane's current betrothed. She appeared as a dark silhouette. The girl on the right was a blue-eyed, vivacious blond in living color with a smile that brought joy to my heart. This had never happened to me before, and I thought I must be dreaming. I tucked it away in my mental file, but I thought about it a lot.

As the wedding of our son drew nearer, I became more apprehensive. I prayed for the Lord to intervene if this was not the best for our son.

Two weeks before the wedding was to take place, Lane's fiancée called the whole thing off! I felt sorry for him, but in my heart I knew God had to be working. My prayers bombarded heaven for his peace and for the "right" one to come along.

Amidst the heartbreak of his breakup, he continued working on his college degree. Two years passed, and I prayed daily for Lane. With graduation near, Lane called to give us the time and details.

We talked of our pride in him as we drove the two hours to his campus. We arrived at his apartment, and he told us to wait while he went to pick up a friend he had invited. Twenty minutes later, our son walked in with a beautiful, blue-eyed blond. I gasped when I saw her. She was the very same girl I had seen in my vision two years earlier. I could hardly contain myself, but kept my mouth closed for fear I would scare them both off.

Their friendship grew from May to November. Our son called us one day and said, "What are you doing November 19? Would you like to go to a wedding?" The rest is history.

This blue-eyed, beautiful blond is everything the Lord showed me and more. Kari is the most wonderful wife and the mother of my two beautiful granddaughters. Our relationship reminds me of Ruth in the Bible and Ruth's mother-in-law, Naomi. So that is what we call each other, "Kari Ruth and Joan Naomi."

The Lord allowed me to see her in my prayer two years before I met her, and then answered my prayer by bringing her into our lives. I know where my Kari Ruth came from!

Showing our child that prayer can help in any situation is a powerful message. Marcia did not think twice about the problem being too strange or difficult. She simply prayed.

✌ *One Quick Prayer* ✌

BY MARCIA ALICE MITCHELL, SALEM, OREGON

I heard a knock at our back door. "Ma'am, is the blue car in the driveway yours?" the old man asked as I dried my hands. I had just cleaned up the kitchen after dinner. My nine-year-old son played on the floor of the living room with his toys spread all around him.

"Yes," I answered, as I wondered what was wrong.

"I thought you'd like to know there's water all over the ground under your car."

"Thanks," I answered. He ambled off to finish his walk, and I panicked.

"What am I going to do?" Despite the fact I was 30 years old, I had just learned to drive and had purchased my first car only a month before. It was an old car with over 100,000 miles already on it. I knew nothing about cars except how to drive one.

A single parent, I had recently moved to this city with my son. The only people we knew were my brother and his family, who were out of town for a few days, and Rex, a young man who had worked with me in the junior high department of our church the year before.

I had to get to work the next day. What was I going to do?

I thought of calling a gas station mechanic, but I had heard too many stories about how women who know little about cars can sometimes be taken advantage of.

My next thought was to phone Rex, but his number was not listed in the phone book. There was only one thing I could do: pray! It was only one short, quick prayer: "Lord, please send Rex."

I sensed assurance from God that Rex would come. Then I did something I had never done before. I acted on my prayer. I turned to my son and told him, "You'd better clean up your toys. Rex is coming over."

"How do you know?" he asked.

"Because I prayed and asked God to send him."

Wide-eyed, he began to pick up his toys.

Forty-five minutes later when the doorbell rang, I knew it could only be one person. I could have hugged Rex when I opened the door, but I didn't think he would understand. Instead, I simply invited him to come in.

"Is your brother here by any chance?" he asked.

I didn't care what his reason was. I knew God had sent him. We talked for a few minutes, and then I asked, "Do you know why there would be a lot of water under my car?"

Rex checked and found a ruptured water hose. Ten minutes before the auto parts store closed, Rex, the last customer of the day, got the hose and replaced the damaged one.

My faith in prayer became a lot stronger that night. This not only helped me believe more in the promises of God, but also helped a nine-year-old-boy discover that God does care about the little things and He does answer prayer. The next time something came up, my son was the one to suggest, "Mom, we need to pray about this— now!"

> A child leaving home, especially under adverse circumstances, can be a difficult time for a mom. Left alone with many questions, Jeanne finds that prayer is the only answer.

◡ *Mom, I'm Moving Out!* ◡

BY JEANNE GETZ PALLOS, LAGUNA NIGUEL, CALIFORNIA

"You and your daughter are so close," the salesclerk said, as she led us to the fitting room. "You seem to have such a great relationship."

Christy, the treasure of my heart, I thought. "Yes," I said, "we're very fortunate."

But a year ago, I wanted to say, *she was not speaking to me. I did not know if she would ever speak to me again.*

When I was hospitalized in 1989 for depression, ten-year-old Christy became the adult. She rose early each morning, made her older brother's lunch, and kept the household running. "My childhood ended when you went into the hospital," she told me years later.

"Christy's so strong," teachers and friends said. It was a good thing. After I came out of the hospital, I spent an hour a week in a therapy group sorting out my childhood injuries, anger, and depression. It was a struggle to go home, be a parent, and function in the so-called normal world. Most of the time I slept.

By Christy's seventeenth birthday, I felt strong. The therapy groups had ended, and my depression was less frequent. Sure, our lives were not perfect, but since my hospitalization, I had worked hard to make up for my mistakes as a parent. The therapist's words haunted me: "You're using Christy to meet your emotional needs. She is not your parent. You are her parent."

The memory of her seventeenth birthday played back in my mind. Things between us had been strained. I battled with depression and illness, as her dad and I struggled in our marriage.

I had bought flowers and a cake. Balloons filled the family room. Yes, things with Christy were strained, but I would show her what a good mother I could be.

"Mom, you never buy me cakes with funny things on them," she complained. "You always buy funny cakes for Jimmy." This year would be different. I studied the birthday themes in the bakery book and picked a cute purple dinosaur for Christy's cake. *She'll love it,* I thought.

After picking up the cake at the bakery, I drove to my husband's office where Christy worked. *I will surprise her,* I thought, *and she can share the cake with her friends at work.*

Walking into the office with flowers and a cake, I put the box in front of Christy. The other workers gathered round to watch her open the lid. "Mom," she said with disgust, "this cake is for a three-year-old. You picked Barney! Do you know who he is?"

I had no idea.

"This is for little kids. How old do you think I am?"

"But I thought you wanted something like I get for Jimmy," I said.

"Yeah, but not something you'd buy a two-year-old!" My insides burned with embarrassment. How could I have been so stupid? I blew it again.

I walked out of the office carrying the flowers and cake. An hour later Christy came home, but we hardly spoke. When her dad came home, she handed us a letter:

> Dear Mom and Dad,
>
> I want you to know I'm moving out. Dad keeps telling me to move out if I don't like his rules, so I've decided to live with a friend. I don't want to hurt you, but I need a break from our family....I don't want you to know where I'm going....I will be in touch when I'm ready.
>
> Love,
> Christy

Was this some kind of joke? Minutes later a friend picked her up, and she walked out of our lives. The cake sat uncut in the refrigerator. The balloons and flowers filled the empty house. Her car sat in the driveway.

"She'll be back," friends said, trying to console me.

Finally the phone call came. "I'm fine," she said in a cold voice. "I'm staying with a friend's family."

My husband panicked and called the police. "Nothing we can do," they said. "By law, a seventeen-year-old can live wherever she wants, as long as she's safe." At least we knew she was safe and living with a family.

A few weeks later, Christy agreed to meet us for therapy, but only on her terms. A very cold, emotionless daughter walked into the room where we sat with a counselor she had chosen. Someone who was on her side, I figured. I immediately hated the therapist.

Then the therapist invited my husband to join Christy in weekly therapy. I was not included.

My world shattered. How could I live without my daughter?

"They always come back," a friend at church said. "My daughter didn't speak to me for three years." Nothing comforted my broken heart.

Six months passed. I was excluded from her junior prom. She invited her dad to take pictures. A brief, impersonal note came on Mother's Day. When our paths crossed, she avoided me or treated me like a stranger.

Was she hurting as much as I was? I wondered.

Just before Christmas, my husband called from work. "Christy's been in a car accident," he said. "It's nothing serious, but she needs to move home so you can drive her to school and to work. She totaled her car."

At least she'll be home, I thought, knowing it would be difficult.

After weeks of being treated coldly, I approached her. "Christy, you've told everyone why you are angry with me, but you haven't told me. I need to know."

"I haven't told you because I don't want to hurt you," she said.

"Not telling me hurts me more. I want to know."

Tears flowed, and years of pain, hurt, and disappointment poured from her heart. "You were never there for me when I was growing up," she said. "You were always sick or in bed."

What do you mean I wasn't there for you? I wanted to scream. *I was always there for you.* But I knew I hadn't been there for her emotionally. She had been the strong, self-sufficient child, the one I didn't think needed my attention.

"I felt like I had to raise myself," she continued.

When she finished, I said, "You're right. I was there for you physically, but I wasn't there for you emotionally. I'm sorry."

"I know you did your best," she said, leaning against the kitchen counter. "I was afraid of hurting you."

"Christy, it's not your job to take care of me," I assured her. "I was the one who was wrong."

"You don't know how hard it was for me to move out," she said. "But I had to do it."

"I admired your courage," I said, meaning it. "And I respect you for what you are sharing with me. You are right about your childhood. Everything you are saying is true."

"You couldn't help it," she said.

"That doesn't matter. I'm so sorry for hurting you. If and when you are ready, I hope you can forgive me."

We hugged, and I kissed her cheek.

Later she said, "Mom, that's all I needed to hear from you. I just needed to know you understood." Our relationship began to heal.

Back in the fitting room of the department store, we giggled and laughed like old friends—no, like mother and daughter. It was a relationship I hoped to never violate again.

"You're so lucky," the salesclerk said as she rang up our purchases. "You two are so close."

Not lucky, I thought. *Blessed.* God had answered my prayers and restored my daughter to me.

7
When God Says No

Taking a child for immunizations has to be one of the harder things a parent does. Those big eyes fill with tears, the bottom lip quivers, and you have to look at that face you love dearly and say, "No. I won't let you skip the shots. You need them." The shot hurts for a moment, but the alternative is much worse: sickness, longer-lasting pain, possibly irreparable damage or death.

When God tells us, "No, you have to go through this," it can feel like we have been deserted or He is inflicting pain. But God knows the plans He has for each of us—plans that take into account what we need to learn to become like Him. When God says no, can you trust Him in this? Can you remember it is not what we see and feel, but what we know is true? His way is perfect. Ours is not. He is God. I am not, and you are not. Think about it for a minute. Really, isn't that a relief?

As for God, his way is perfect; the word of the LORD is flawless.
He is a shield for all who take refuge in him.

Psalm 18:30

167

The loss of a child can be the most devastating event a mom can face. With a strong faith in God and the power of prayer, a mom can find it's possible to handle all things.

∽ Timmy's Ring ∽

BY NANCY C. ANDERSON, HUNTINGTON BEACH, CALIFORNIA

"What a lovely ring. It looks like an antique." My new neighbor touched my hand and said, "It's so unusual. Where did you get it?"

"I had it custom made."

"I have a friend who's a jeweler. Would you mind if I copied it?" she asked.

I smiled at her. "First let me tell you the story behind the design."

∽

It was just after New Year's Day in 1990 when I found out I was pregnant with our second child. Ron, my husband, was thrilled. I was apprehensive. Nick, our five-year-old, had several learning disabilities and was quite a handful. I told Ron, "I am afraid I won't have enough energy to take care of Nick and a newborn baby."

Through all the required checkups, my doctor assured me everything was fine. However, since I would be 35 when the baby was born, it meant I had a higher chance of having a baby with birth defects. My doctor decided to do an ultrasound.

I tried to find a comfortable spot on the hard examination table as the nurse's aide squirted the cold sonogram gel on my expanding belly. One technician slid the scope over my stomach as the other one watched the monitor. I looked at the woman who was watching my baby on the screen. Her face didn't have much expression. Then suddenly, it did.

Her eyes widened and her hands flew involuntarily to her mouth as she made a sad squeaking sound. "What's wrong?" I asked. I sat up and repeated my question. She tried to compose herself as she scurried toward the door and whispered, "I'm sorry." The other technician left, too. I tumbled off the table and went to look at the picture that was still on the screen. I didn't see anything unusual. To me it just looked like a blurry negative of a skinny baby. I looked down at my stomach and rubbed it as I whispered a prayer. "Oh Lord, I think we're in trouble. Please help us."

My doctor ordered an amniocentesis test performed after seeing the ultrasound. After the results of the test came in, we went back to the hospital for the results. The doctor solemnly entered the room. In a voice that was extremely clinical in nature, he gave us a brief synopsis of "Trisomy 18."

"What your unborn child has is a genetic disorder that always involves profound mental retardation and severe disfigurements." Then he said the words that still live inside a tiny, zipped pocket of my heart: "Your baby's condition is usually incompatible with life. Most women in your position choose to get an abortion in order to spare themselves unnecessary anguish. We can schedule yours for tomorrow morning."

I wasn't able to speak, since I had stopped breathing. I felt like I was drowning. I wanted to drift down into the cool dark water and disappear. A silent tear slid down my face, and we left the office without a word.

That afternoon I prayed, "Lord, I believe abortion is wrong, but I don't want to go through 'unnecessary anguish.' On my own, I don't have the strength to fall in love with a baby who is going to die. Please show me how."

As I prayed, I remembered that the Lord could have chosen to avoid the horrific anguish of the cross. What if He had taken the easy way out? I saw that the value of His gift was measured by the greatness of His suffering. I told the Lord with renewed strength, "I offer my pain to You as a gift. I will not abort this child."

I kept saying it, even before I meant it: "I choose to love this baby with all my heart." I willed my words into actions. In faith I moved my hands as I timidly caressed my stomach. In faith I moved my lips as I mouthed the words, "I love you." No sound came out. I kept repeating the phrase until my brain found the secret passageway to my heart, and I was free to taste the bittersweet tears of loving a child who would never love me.

My mother said, "Try not to think about the future. Your baby is alive today. Be alive with him and treasure every moment."

I talked to him, sang lullabies to him, and gave him gentle massages through my skin. I knew that I would have to do my best mothering before he was born. Each day I prayed, "Lord, please let him live long enough to know that he is loved. Let us have time to kiss him hello and kiss him good-bye. Let his life be free of pain and full of love. Please, Lord, give us the strength to bear this overwhelming burden."

Four months later, we met little Timmy face-to-face. The nurse covered his fragile, one-pound, four-ounce body in a soft blue blanket and matching cap. His heart monitor beeped an unsteady greeting as she handed him to me.

His beautiful little rosebud mouth surprised me. It was an oasis of perfection. We held our emotions in check, knowing we had to pour a lifetime of love into a minuscule cup. Ron and I took turns rocking him as we kissed his soft cheek. We repeatedly told him, "We love you, Timmy." He never opened his eyes. He felt no pain as his heartbeat got slower and slower, and then reluctantly stopped.

We kissed him good-bye and introduced him, through prayer, to his heavenly Father, "Lord, here is our son. Thank You for the gift of his precious life and for the privilege of being his parents. We release him into Your healing arms. Thank You for answering our prayers. Amen."

Then we cried.

❦

I looked at my neighbor's tear-stained face and said, "I had this ring made a few days after his birth. I drew a picture of what I wanted, told the jeweler why I wanted it, and he worked late into the night to have it for me the next day."

She looked closer as I explained the design. "See the two curved bands of gold? The longer one symbolizes my husband's arm and the smaller band represents mine. Our 'arms' are holding a small lavender alexandrite. This is Timmy's birthstone."

She was silent for a long time and finally said, "You should be the only person in the world to wear that ring. I wouldn't dream of copying it now. Tell me about the diamonds."

"There are 13 tiny diamonds, one precious jewel for each minute he was alive. I wear it on my 'baby' finger so he is always with me."

"For you created my inmost being; you knit me together in my mother's womb. I praise you because I am fearfully and wonderfully made" (Psalm 139:13-14).

Lucinda had very specific requests of God. She took the Scripture verse, "Present your requests to God" very seriously. So why then did the Lord let her down? Lucinda found out just why the Lord said no to her requests.

∿ When God's Answer Is No ∿

BY LUCINDA SECREST MCDOWELL, WETHERSFIELD, CONNECTICUT

The year was 1976. Our country was celebrating its bicentennial, and I was a young 23, busily laying my life plans before the Lord.

I had long ago decided what I wanted to be when I grew up and with whom I wanted to spend the rest of my life. All I needed was for God to answer my prayers. And by that I meant answer yes to my prayers, specifically to *this* prayer:

> God, all I want to do is marry Paul and live the rest of my days right here in the beautiful Blue Ridge Mountains. We could build a log house right here on his land and raise our children in the country. I will even teach Bible studies for my church if You want me to. But please, please, please answer this prayer, and I will spend the rest of my life serving you here in North Carolina!

I didn't exactly view God as a cosmic Santa Claus who ponied up with the loot after reviewing my list of gimmes, but I was close. Hadn't I waited for this godly man before falling in love? Hadn't I finished college and worked for several years while volunteering as a church youth leader? Hadn't I prayed for God to guide and direct me?

Yes to all of the above! So I was finally confident that my plan A would work out, and I would enjoy some version of "happily ever after."

God *did* answer my prayer.

He said no.

In fact, He said no to all of it: Paul, the mountains, the house, the kids, the country life, and North Carolina.

I believe that God answers every heartfelt prayer either "yes," "no," or "wait." I love it when I get a "yes" answer and can mark the date in my prayer notebook next to a big PTL! It's a lot harder to get a "wait" answer, but it reminds me to continually bring those concerns and people before Him with prayers of hope.

"No" answers are another thing entirely. There is finality and a reality that must be faced. Dreams die, and pain and confusion are often companions in the aftermath. I felt all these things initially back in 1976 when God said no to my requests.

But I mustered courage to move forward with my life, believing that "no good thing does he withhold from those whose walk is blameless" (Psalm 84:11).

I moved to Boston for a seminary degree. Journalism work then took me to Chicago and Thailand. Then I served as a missions pastor in San Francisco, traveling around the world twice before I was 30. North Carolina seemed very far away, and in the meantime, life held many surprises and challenges.

Today I live in a Connecticut city, not in the Carolina countryside. Mike and I celebrated our twentieth anniversary this year with our two sons and two daughters. Yes, I do lead Bible studies, but I also speak to thousands of people each year both nationally and internationally. This year my fifth book was published.

My life looks nothing like the one I prayed for so long ago. I now realize that one of the reasons God said no was that, for me, that particular vision was too small. To grant those desires would have allowed me to settle for what was comfortable, rather than take risks and stretch beyond my comfort zone to a life that could only be accomplished (and survived) through a daily partnership with God the Father, His Son, Jesus Christ, and through the power of the Holy Spirit.

My world didn't end when God answered my prayers with "no." Instead those losses opened me up to be filled with other people and new experiences.

Yet even today, so many years later, I often catch myself praying only "safe" prayers for my grown children. Then I remember, with a hard-earned wisdom, that God has far more for them than I could even hope or imagine. So I change my prayers to "Your will be done. In the closed doors and opened windows, in the nos as well as the yesses, may they live in Your best."

I'm confident that God answers every heartfelt prayer in His way and in His timing. And in our faith that He is good and in our obedience to His wisdom, we discover joy and a life full of meaning.

While most moms would be crying and cursing God for the tragedy of losing a child, Anne found that Mary and Mike were at peace with the Lord. This was a mystery until she discovered the prayer that let them cope.

A Smile to Remember

BY ANNE C. JOHNSON, KEARNEY, NEBRASKA

A lone tear trickled down Mary's pale cheek. "May I see him?" she whispered.

I attempted to swallow the lump in my throat. Silently I led Mary and Mike to the intensive care room of their son. The couple, whom I guessed to be in their thirties, walked hand in hand behind me. I pulled back the curtain. Tears threatened to tumble down my cheeks.

Brian's little six-year-old body hardly took up a third of the ICU bed. His tiny chest moved up and down in sync with the ventilator.

"Is he breathing?" Mike questioned.

"No, sir, I am sorry," I said. "The tube in his mouth is delivering air to his lungs. That's why his chest is moving."

I felt chills in my heart as the doctor spoke to Mike and Mary. "Your son has suffered severe brain damage from his accident. I am not sure if it occurred when the car hit Brian, or when his body landed on the cement in the parking lot. No matter when it happened, it has made Brian brain-dead."

I tried to focus on the monitor or out the window, but I felt the need to look at Mary. Her blue eyes were wet with tears. She stood silently wringing the tissue in her hands. I don't recall what she wore or any other details about her physical appearance, except her smile and whispered request: "God, please let Brian live just a while longer."

A smile? How could she? What was there to smile about? Didn't she realize that her son was dead? My face felt hot with anger. I couldn't understand Mary's behavior.

Mary and Mike agreed to donate Brian's organs. They kept vigil by Brian's side, and silently waited through the long, grueling hours while Brian's tissue and blood type were tested for compatibility with organ recipients.

Though Brian's brain was dead, my job was to make sure the rest of his organs continued to function, so another child might receive the hope of a better life. I was so wrapped up in the busyness of the doctors' orders, I did not allow myself to think about Mary's smile.

The hour before Brian went to surgery to remove his donor organs for transplanting into recipients, I walked in the room to find his mother lying on the bed next to him. While she stroked his blond, curly hair, she whispered, "I thank God for the time I got to spend with you. I will miss you something awful, but honey, this gift you are giving other children will allow their families time to spend with them."

The floodgates were open, and tears fell freely down my cheeks. I now fully understood why Mary had smiled. She had peace in her heart. In the midst of tragedy, she was able to see God's hand at work in her life.

With a nod of her head, Mary acknowledged I had come into the room. I felt intrusive watching something so beautiful and intimate.

Without a second thought, I knelt beside the bed and prayed for Mary and her family. Mary's soft voice penetrated the depths of my heart: "Thank You, God, for answering my prayer. Though I will never hold my baby again, Brian will live on in the gifts he is giving to other children."

My shift ended much as it had begun, with charting and paperwork. However, I couldn't escape the image of Mary's lovely smile as she held the hand of her dead child. The smile that first infuriated me is now permanently imprinted on my heart, for it's a symbol of peace and compassion from God.

When our child is in pain and hurting, our only prayer to God is to heal the child, and right now! But Kim found God's negative response the answer to an unknown blessing.

∿ *Sometimes God Says No* ∿

BY KIM VOGEL SAWYER, HUTCHINSON, KANSAS

"Surgery?" I could hardly believe what I was hearing. Six months ago, I took my oldest daughter, Kristian, for a visit to the gynecologist. She was suffering from severe abdominal pain, and I was becoming increasingly concerned. A sonogram revealed several cysts on her left ovary, and the doctor said they were common in girls Kristian's age.

"In all likelihood, they'll clear up on their own, eliminating her pain." He told us to come back for a follow-up visit and another sonogram in six months.

The follow-up sonogram showed that not only had Kristian's previous cysts grown, but new ones had formed. Surgery was the only solution.

As Kristian and I left the doctor's office, I offered cheerful words to ease my daughter's fears, but inwardly I fumed. Hadn't I prayed consistently for Kristian to be healed of this discomfort? Why hadn't God answered? *God, weren't You listening? She needs to be focusing on her college work, not worrying about surgery,* my thoughts railed.

The day of Kristian's surgery, I took her to the hospital, stayed with her until the anesthesia took effect, and then headed to the waiting room.

"The surgery will only take about 45 minutes. I will come and get you when Kristian is moved to recovery." The doctor walked through the double doors leading to my daughter.

You know, God, if You had just answered my prayers, I could be at work right now giving that social studies test to my fifth-graders, and Kristian could be keeping up with notes in her college classes. My hand quivered while I tried to pass the time grading fifth-grade essays. *Was it too much to ask for You to clear up a few little cysts?*

Forty-five minutes passed and I packed my things, ready to join Kristian in her recovery room. An hour slipped by, then an hour and a half, and still no one came to get me. My prayers took on a different tone. *God, what are they doing back there? What's taking so long? Is everything okay?*

After two hours passed, I approached the receptionist's desk. "My daughter has been in surgery twice as long as expected. Is there any way I can find out what's going on?"

She made a call to the operating room, and a message came back: "The doctor has found something else, and she's trying to take care of it."

"Something else?" I sank back into my chair, reeling in fear and uncertainty. No more complaining, no more questioning, now I simply begged. *Please, God, be with my daughter. Whatever is wrong, let the doctor be able to fix it."*

After three and a half hours of waiting and worrying, the surgeon finally walked through the double doors. She showed me pictures of Kristian's ovaries and uterus, covered with bright-red patches of endometriosis. Little wonder my daughter had been uncomfortable.

"Endometriosis is a very painful condition, and it can have devastating side effects, including infertility," the doctor explained. "It's a good thing we discovered this. I would have never expected it in someone Kristian's age, and sonograms are useless in detecting it. The only way we could have possibly detected it was by surgery. I burned off as much as I could, and we'll treat your daughter with medication to keep more from growing."

The doctor's words, "The only way we could have possibly detected it was by surgery" repeated several times over in my mind, followed by the realization that if they hadn't found the endometriosis, it would have continued growing with serious consequences.

Tears filled my eyes as I realized that God had answered my prayers to heal Kristian's cysts. He had answered with a resounding No. And now I understood why. God knew what was happening inside my daughter's body, and He knew it needed to be dealt with. How grateful I was that the surgery had taken place.

The same gratefulness washes over me again every time I hold a precious little person in my arms: Conner Jayden, born three years after Kristian's surgery. His name holds rich significance. Conner means "much wanted," and Jayden means "God has heard." When I look into his sweet face, I thank God for not healing the cysts that led the doctor to perform the surgery. My grandson is evidence of God's wisdom and unrelenting love.

Sometimes, God says no. When He does, I have learned it is for my own good, and I thank Him for the answers to every unique situation.

Raising a child means a daily round of prayers to the Lord: prayers to watch over our child, prayers for guidance, and even prayers for patience! Amy found out just how much she herself learned as she prayed for Heather.

⌣ *For This Child* ⌣

BY AMY WALLACE, LAWRENCEVILLE, GEORGIA

In July of 2000 God blessed me with a second child—a baby daughter who was prayed for from conception and loved greatly. Hannah was a whirlwind of a child, destined to teach her mommy much about the power of prayer. And as active as she was, prayer proved exactly what we needed.

At six months this child decided she should walk. Nothing detoured her: not the falls, not the boo-boos, not my praying for contentment with crawling. I couldn't keep up with this little one, and I cringed every time she took off after her big sister.

So I prayed.

I asked God to protect her, to keep her safe, and to give us wisdom. And feeling all the bruises and strains from catching her and trying to keep up with her, I added a number of prayers for my own safety and health so I could be the best mommy possible to this energetic child. A solution I considered to protect the both of us involved tying pillows around Hannah during her waking hours—an idea my husband rejected. He reminded me to trust God and keep praying.

So I did.

Then, with a profusely bleeding gash on her head from a fall, Hannah presented me with my first experience in a pediatric emergency room. Hannah left the emergency room with nothing more than a bandage. But nothing could bandage the pain in my heart. I began to doubt God's protection. I doubted my abilities as a mother. I doubted that God would keep us from serious harm. I doubted He was listening to my prayers.

I tried to remember how God had answered in the past. Because I'm diabetic, both of my pregnancies had been difficult and filled with opportunities for fear. As I prayed, God challenged me to trust Him with my health.

Through Hannah, God revealed how to trust Him with my child.

One beautiful spring day, right before nap time, we were outside. Elizabeth, my four-year-old, and Hannah, then 18 months old, played happily on the front porch. I rounded the corner of our garage and walked up the concrete sidewalk to join in the pretend picnic by our porch swing. But Hannah didn't wait for my arrival and began to toddle down the three porch stairs. She missed the first step, and all I could envision was her hitting the concrete, face first.

Everything happened in slow motion and, in a flash, all at the same time. I knew I couldn't get to her and doubted God would intervene.

I sent up an urgent prayer anyway.

I still have no idea how I managed to get under Hannah and break her fall.

I take that back. I do know.

God. He showed me the literal meaning of Godspeed!

That day I took Hannah's place in the emergency room.

The doctors X-rayed my foot and determined I had ruptured a tendon and fractured a joint. Three podiatrists, two casts, and one surgery later, I was finally on the road to recovery.

Every time Hannah looked at my purple cast, she cried. I prayed. Nothing helped until I told Hannah, "God used Mommy to protect you, and Mommy will be okay." Still she looked sad. So I added, "Honey, I would do it all again, just to keep you safe."

For six weeks after the surgery, I would look down at my purple cast and remember the priceless lesson I had learned. While God said no to the request for my health and safety, He enabled me to play a part in protecting my child. In truth, God answered more than my prayers. He answered my deepest need by showing us all a picture of His self-sacrificing love.

What a joy to know God answers prayer in unexpected ways. In His perfect wisdom He also engineers the U-turns from doubt to faith the very moment we pray!

Now when I look at the small scar on my foot, I smile. I remember that God will do exceedingly abundantly over and above all I can ask or imagine—not only for me, but for my children as well.

For our children to outlive us is a mom's greatest prayer. The Lord may sometimes say no to this request. Through God, Jennifer found enough love to last a lifetime.

∿ A Legacy of Giving ∿

BY JENNIFER LYNN CARY, PHOENIX, ARIZONA

There was once this boy who lived with his three sisters and his parents and his dog, Jack—can't forget about Jack. He loved that dog. This boy was like most other boys nearing their teens. He had a killer set of Legos and loved to draw airplanes and jet bombers. He was crazy over hockey and wrestling, practicing moves on his sisters. He bent the truth every now and again, especially if it redirected the trouble toward one of his sisters. This boy was a normal, average boy.

But he was also very special and unique. He gave his heart to Jesus when he was ten years old. And though he often acted like an everyday type of boy, he was one of a kind, fearfully and wonderfully made with a tender heart and a generous spirit.

Then one day he did what was very normal and average for a young teen. For the first time in his life, he accepted a babysitting job. Friends of his parents wanted to look at a possible new church site for the congregation. They asked him to come over, play some games, and watch TV with their nine-year-old daughter. It took all of an hour and a half, and he walked away with five whole dollars.

Five whole dollars doesn't sound like much, but it changed the lives of hundreds of people.

The following Sunday, after his pastor made a request for prayers for guidance as the church considered plans for expanding, the boy tracked down the pastor and handed over the five whole dollars with the words, "Whatever we end up doing, we will need a building fund. You can put this towards it."

Pastor Steve's heart was moved. Here in his hand was the first answer to his prayer. In fact, he was so moved that he shared the story with the congregation, much to the boy's embarrassment. And then the congregation was so moved that they pledged enough money to pay off all the debts and build a much-needed sanctuary so everyone could worship together.

Five whole years and many prayers later, the congregation moved into their new sanctuary. But they moved in without the boy.

You see, he was special in one more way. Born with cystic fibrosis, he went home to heaven when he was only 15. The congregation had poured out prayers for healing, but in the end he still died.

I, too, prayed for this young man to be healed. Countless tears were shed as I knelt at God's feet, begging for his life. But God said no. He had a plan far beyond that which I could see or truly understand. This boy's life on earth was short, but intensely meaningful.

At the memorial service, in the very gym where the congregation had worshiped, the line was so long that the service was delayed for 15 minutes. Extra chairs were set up, and still there were people who stood for over two hours to pay their respects to this teenage boy who thought he was nothing special. During the service, people shared words of remembrance. From five-year-olds to ninety-five-year-olds, this special boy had touched them all. And though it did seem for a time that their prayers and mine had not been heard, healings in hearts, people leaning on Christ, and the hope that burned deep inside clearly told us our boy was now whole. Our prayers had been answered.

Today his legacy of giving lives on. Many walk into that new sanctuary thinking of the boy and how God multiplied five whole dollars. It can make you wonder how many other people think they are not special, that their gifts are not needed, or that their prayers are not heard.

But that's only part of this boy's legacy. He didn't think he was special. He didn't know he had the gift of encouragement. Yet his spirit of generosity and example of trust touched countless teens and adults alike. Hundreds of people of all ages benefit every Sunday from that sacrifice so readily given. And if you pull back the carpet throughout the building, you will find prayers, poured out in ink over concrete, to be literally a part of the foundation, as if etched in stone.

God took a normal, everyday boy and poured His heart into him so that the hearts of many could be moved. And even though the boy has gone to his eternal home, God is still moving hearts in a building and answering prayers the boy could have only imagined. His legacy will live on, and that legacy is something I especially hold near and dear to my heart. His caring nature and willingness to share make me grateful to God for my close relationship with him, even for such a brief time. When my time comes and the Lord takes me home, I will see this boy once again. I am thankful for that assurance.

This story might sound like a made-up, feel-good movie-of-the-week or another "loaves and fishes" parable. But that is the most exciting part: Every single word is true.

I know.

The boy's name is Ian. He is my son.

Moms often pray for the safety and health of their unborn child. Most times, to their great joy, their prayers are answered. Sometimes it takes a while to find out why the Lord answers no.

⌁ *Day of No Ashes* ⌁

BY GINGER K. NELSON, HUNTSVILLE, ALABAMA

"Congratulations! You have a baby boy!" Our third child entered the world on Ash Wednesday, 1967.

My husband and I rejoiced over Danny's birth until the pediatrician walked in. He introduced himself and then informed us that our son had all the signs of Down syndrome. His wide-set, almond-shaped eyes and simian crease across his palm were just a few symptoms of the chromosome anomaly. A few more tests would be needed to make a firm diagnosis.

"People with this syndrome have mild to moderate mental retardation." The doctor's words rang loudly, and silence preceded the questions that spilled from our lips as we tried to understand this labyrinth of unsorted and unfathomable details.

My husband, Fritz, tried to encourage me. "Just think, Danny will always be with us. When the others move out on their own, we'll still have our special boy."

When Fritz left the hospital room, thoughts flooded my mind, keeping me from the rest I desperately needed. "God, what will my parents say? How will our friends and neighbors react? And what if I don't love him enough? God, where are You? I feel so alone."

I telephoned the hospital chaplain's office to ask if he would bring the ashes I always receive on the first day of Lent. I planned to ask him where God was when all this happened and how I was supposed to handle the situation, but he never came. No ashes, no answers. I was afraid.

I watched the other new mothers walk to the nursery and bring their babies back to cuddle with, coo to, and caress. I closed my door. Moments later, a nurse carrying an infant wrapped in a hospital receiving blanket walked into my room. "I thought you might like to hold him," she suggested. She placed him into my arms and left.

Warmth radiated through me as I gazed at Danny's innocent face. I truly saw the person God had given us to raise. Of course I loved him enough. "Thank You, God, for being with me. I know You'll be here every minute of every day. Thank You for the time when I do not have the strength to walk another minute. I know You will carry me." I pulled my sweet son closer and cried tears of joy.

I knew from that moment forward that, with God's help, I would be the best possible mother for Danny, and Fritz would be a wonderful dad.

Other people have often questioned how I made such a sudden change in my life, but one look at my helpless infant told me all I needed to know. All my doubts of raising this special child disappeared. My question of whether I would love him enough was answered immediately, as the nurse placed my son in my arms.

I had prayed for a healthy baby; he was. I had prayed to be a loving mother; I was. I prayed that even a baby with special needs could benefit from my caring; he did.

With God beside me, I knew I could face the world with all its negative expectations of a child with Down syndrome, and I never looked back. Never again did I ask the Lord if I would love him enough. Danny has taught me more about the love of God than I could have imagined on the day of no ashes.

My husband and I had a great opportunity. We seized it and did our best to raise our son to be a Christian. He has never disappointed us, and I'm sure Danny has never disappointed God.

8

Praying on a Mom's Behalf

Remember that vow you made when you were a child? I'll bet you do. It probably went something like, "I'll never do that to my kid!" or "I'll never say that to my child!" or…You fill in the specifics. And then God's sense of humor shines through, and invariably we end up with a child very much like ourselves. Yep, suddenly we get a better idea of what our mothers went through raising us. And sometimes it's not a very pretty picture. So when those "I've turned into my mother" or "Please, God, don't let me turn into my mother" moments dawn on you, may I offer a suggestion? Pray for your mother. No matter how horrible or wonderful she was, you are living and breathing now because she gave you birth. Ask Him to bless your mother. Be grateful for the life lessons learned that keep you from the same mistakes she made, maybe even breaking damaging cycles generations long. And when your child announces, "I will never do that to my kid," smile, bite your tongue, and pray for your mom.

*These should learn first of all to put their religion into practice
by caring for their own family and so repaying their parents and
grandparents, for this is pleasing to God.*

1 Timothy 5:4

There are times in many of our lives where we find ourselves praying for someone who is, or will soon be, a mom. God listens to these prayers, too! Toña is very thankful that He does.

◡: God's Unlikely Expert :◞

BY TOÑA MORALES-CALKINS, SANTA ROSA, CALIFORNIA

"God, I shouldn't be the expert here. All I know about childbirth is what I've seen in films and from our class discussion on how to do it. I've never even seen a live birth other than kittens! And now I'm the expert? Help me know what to do."

I prayed desperately as I got my first-aid kit and blanket from the back of my car. Closing the hatchback on my Toyota, I trotted through the pouring rain to the car ahead of mine. I looked back down the empty road toward the mud slide that had cut us off in that direction, desperately hoping that somebody more knowledgeable than I would be driving toward us. It had been raining almost daily for over a month, and there was flooding and mud slides everywhere. Even as I looked, I knew it would be hours before rescue crews got to us.

"Here's a blanket, Pete. Spread it on the backseat for her," I said, trying to sound like I knew what I was doing. "And put the first-aid kit on the driver's seat for me, would you?" I handed the items to him and turned toward the front passenger's side of the car. "Okay, Sarah, I'm back." I opened the door. "How are you doing?"

In reply she looked at me and continued to breathe in short pants. Her face and eyes showed the pain she was in and the tension she felt. She reached out with her right hand and gripped my arm hard. We stayed that way until the contraction eased and she released her hold on me. "Pete's got the blanket in the back now. Can you move?"

"That was a strong one. I think we'd better hurry," she gasped, trying to get her breathing to return to normal. "But I don't know if I can stand up." Her eyes flashed apology to me, and my heart cried out again to God for help. These first-time parents and their baby deserved better care than they could possibly get from me. I was an 18-year-old disaster volunteer, en route to her first assignment.

"Pete and I will help you," I told her, turning to look at her husband, who had come around to this side of the car. "Right?" He nodded grimly and stepped forward to help his wife. Once standing, she leaned on both of us as we shut the front door and opened the back one. We got her seated just as the next contraction hit.

"So you've done this a lot, being with the Red Cross, right?" Pete asked nervously. "You know exactly what to do in case there's a problem, right?" Though I wanted to give him the reassurance he sought, I knew better than to lie.

"No, I haven't ever done this before. But I have had enough training to get us through this. With God watching over all of us, it will be okay." Pete and I looked in unison at the muddy hillside high above the road, and then back to the chunk of it that had blocked our passage when it slid down over the pavement. That chunk of hillside was higher than the top of his car. Looking at each other again, we both knew God had been watching earlier when it fell in front of their car and not on top of it.

"Can you help me scoot back now?" Sarah called our focus back again. "I think I need to lie down." Lying down in the backseat of their Chevy was not regal comfort, but it was better than sitting up in the front seat. "Sarah?" I asked tentatively, "would you mind if I took a look now?" I wondered whether I would know what I was looking at as I bent forward.

"Argh! Pete, hold my hand!" she called out as the next contraction hit. I watched in wonder as the top of a little head, covered with brown or black hair, entered my view.

"I see the top of the head!" I called out excitedly. "The baby's crowning!"

The head disappeared again as the contraction passed. I took a deep breath and tried to sound confident as I spoke to them. "Okay, we're getting close now. Pete, you do whatever Sarah asks you to, and Sarah, you do whatever you need to, to handle the pain."

"What are you going to do?" Pete asked.

"Nothing, I hope. If everything goes as planned, I will just be here to clean off the baby and wrap him or her in the blanket Sarah brought with you. She'll be doing all the work." Sarah smiled at me then, and I was amazed at her courage and calm.

"We'll be fine," she reassured us. "Just think, it could have been you over there, Pete," she said, indicating me with a nod of her head. She laughed as he blanched. "He gets woozy just thinking about it. He nearly fainted when the doctor showed us a video of a real birth. I am so glad you're here," she told me.

Hoping that I would live up to her confidence in me, I reached for the newspaper in the front seat and laid out a shoestring from my first-aid kit in front of me. "Ungh," she gasped again, as the pain came on strong. "I want to push."

"Then do it," I said as I watched the little head come into view again. "Just do it." Frantically, I tried to recall whether that was the right advice. The baby's head slowly appeared. I had to remind myself to breathe as I watched it happen. "Push more, Sarah," I told her as first one shoulder appeared and then the other.

"I can't do it anymore. I need to rest," she pleaded. Her hand was white as it tightly gripped Pete's. I could see him gritting his teeth in pain.

"Just a little longer," I encouraged. "Just a little more. The baby's almost here."

Sarah obliged with one last, long, strong push. It seemed to me the baby practically leapt into my waiting hands. Supporting the head, I pulled gently until the baby's feet came free of his mother.

"It's a boy!" My hands were shaking as I grabbed the newspaper and started to clean off some of the blood and fluid from the baby's head.

"Is he okay? Why isn't he crying?" Pete's anguished voice sounded just before his son's first wail. "Thank God—he's alive," Pete said as a relieved smile took over his face. "I have a son!" He moved over the seat to kiss Sarah, who smiled wearily.

For the first time, I felt waterlogged as the rain soaked into my clothing. I was kneeling on the muddy roadway outside the car during the birth, unaware of anything except the miracle unfolding in the backseat before me. I picked up the blanket that Sarah had kept with her and wrapped it around her little son. When I put him on his mother's tummy, his crying soon stopped.

She looked down at him, tears filling her eyes. "Oh, he's beautiful," she whispered. "He's so beautiful." Looking at his little face, I was awed to realize what a part I had played in his entry into the world. Wonder and gratitude filled my soul as I said a prayer of thanksgiving to God.

"What's his name?" I asked.

"Michael Peter," Sarah said, "after my dad and his." Little Michael had fallen asleep then, and his mother was soon dozing.

"What do we do now?" Pete asked in a whisper, once I had gotten into the front seat. "We still can't go anywhere. There's no help coming because of the floods."

"We pray," I said. "At least, that's all I know that we can do. God knows we're here. He'll send someone soon."

"You say that like it's true."

"It is true," I affirmed. "God sent me to help you two get through this part, didn't He? He'll send someone else to help the four of us now." We lapsed into silence then, each saying a silent prayer for God's help. Eventually I dozed, lulled by the rhythm of the rain on the roof of the car.

Shortly before sundown, a rescue unit from the local fire department found us. They checked on the mother and baby and pronounced that all was well. They offered us an escort back down the road that had just been cleared. I got into my car and followed behind Pete and the rescue unit to the hospital. Still wet and cold, I waited with Pete until the doctors had finished with Sarah and little Michael. We went in to see them together. As the first relatives began arriving, I told Sarah good-bye.

"Good-bye, Toña," she said. "We'll never forget you or this day. I will keep thanking God you were there when we needed you."

Driving home, I thought back over the afternoon. I had been so upset to see the mud slide, frustrated to miss my first volunteer assignment working at a shelter for the flood victims. When Pete had approached my car, I almost hadn't rolled the window down because of my anger at the situation.

I realized that I hadn't missed my first volunteer assignment after all. God had known *exactly* where I was needed most. I had been the answer to someone's prayer.

As little kids, we include Mom in our nightly prayers, expecting God to answer the innocent requests we make. As adults, we pray differently for the needs of our parents, but still we expect the Lord to provide. We pray for good health, a strong mind, and a sound heart for our aging parents. Carol prayed for companionship for her mom, and God faithfully heard her prayers.

A Roommate for Mom

BY CAROL GENENGELS, SEABECK, WASHINGTON

You can do this! I told myself. *No, I can't!* I argued back. (Once I had actually driven here, parked, then after a moment restarted the car and driven away. I just couldn't do it!)

The contents of my breakfast felt like cement beneath my pounding heart. *Why am I such a chicken anyway?* I asked myself. Gathering my courage, I opened the heavy doors and entered the nursing home. The entrance was cheery enough with Victorian wallpaper, tapestry wing-backed chairs, and potted palms. I swished past the stone-faced person at the receptionist's desk and rounded the corner. I braced myself for the familiar odors: a combination of institutional food, urine, powder, and disinfectants. Pretending I was in a fine art gallery, I focused on the paintings that decorated the long corridors. An elderly gentleman slumped in his wheelchair as an aide pushed him down the hall.

An angry woman yelled as I approached. "Where have you been all this time? Why won't you help me?" Feeling guilty and callous, I ignored her and proceeded toward my destination. Sighing heavily I turned right and counted one, two, three, fourth door on the left, Mom's home for the past two years. A series of health problems rendered her in need of 24-hour care.

She was in bed and her eyes were closed. I studied her still-beautiful face. Mom's once-stylish gray hair was tied at the nape of her neck with a black ribbon. Bending to kiss her, I gently tapped her shoulder. "Mom, are you awake? It's Carol." Her brows furrowed as her pale-blue eyes opened. "Hello, dear," she whispered.

"How are you doing, Mom?" I asked.

"Not very good." Her voice betrayed her loneliness.

I straightened her pillows, as if that would magically make everything better. "Have you seen your doctor lately?"

"No, I don't think so," she whispered. "Carol, I am so lonely. Can you please take me home with you? I would be no trouble at all."

Guilt, my frequent companion, loomed up like an elephant. But there was no way I could take care of my mother. She was unable to walk and had trouble eating and drinking. Besides, my husband and I both worked full-time to put our youngest child through college.

One solace was the fact that Mom's sister, Aunt Marie, resided in the same nursing home. My sister and I begged the directors to let Mom and her sister share a room. They stubbornly refused, insisting they didn't want to disrupt Aunt Marie's routine, as she had a congenial roommate. Besides, they reasoned, Mom and her sister could see each other daily in the dining room.

I began praying for a compatible roommate for Mom. Sadie, the cranky spinster in the next bed, ordered Mom around like a child. She was nearly deaf, and her TV drowned out Mom's television programs. At best they tolerated each other. After a few months, Sadie passed away, and soon Mom had another roommate. The next time I saw Mother, I asked how she liked her new roommate. "I don't!" she answered tersely. "She never shuts up!"

Indeed, Millie babbled around the clock, affording Mom very little sleep. I talked to social services, and Millie was soon relocated to a new room.

Next came Ruby, a severely depressed amputee. She spent most of her days staring into space. My efforts to evoke a smile seldom worked. Ruby just plain didn't like my mom and asked to be transferred to another room. Mom was alone once again. "Lord," I reminded Him, "please hear my prayers and send Mom a roommate who will also be her friend."

The bed next to Mom's remained vacant for weeks. I brought my favorite painting of Jesus smiling at a bird on His outstretched finger. I placed it on the wall opposite Mom's bed so that she could see it at all times. It made her smile.

Feeling guilty once again, I informed Mom that I would be out of town for several days. A week later I tiptoed into Mom's dimly lit room. She appeared to be sleeping. Someone was curled up asleep in the next bed. I quietly pulled the curtain between their beds for some privacy and kissed Mom's forehead. Opening her eyes, she sleepily said my name. "Carol…" She smiled and grasped my hand.

I took a deep breath. "Hi, Mom. How are you feeling?"

"Okay, dear. How are you?"

"I'm fine."

"I missed you."

"I missed you, too, Mom. I see you have a new roommate."

Mom nodded. "Yes!"

"How do you like this roommate?" I asked, fully expecting a negative reply.

"We're good friends!"

"You are?"

"Oh yes! Remember Betty?"

"Betty?"

"Betty O'Rear."

"Your old friend? But…I thought she lived in Montana!" (Mom's best friend had moved away over 20 years ago.)

"She's moved back to be near her son. She's my roommate now!"

I peeked behind the curtain. Age and disease had certainly taken their toll, but Betty's vivacious smile and warm, brown eyes had not changed a bit. I drew back the curtain between their beds. Betty reached her trembling hand toward Mom's outstretched palm. "I am so thankful to be here with Helen!" she said. "We look out for each other, don't we, Rosa?" ("Rosa" was Betty's nickname for Mom.)

"We sure do!" Mom said.

"We've been laughing all day, remembering good old times."

"Yes, we have!" Mom agreed.

Gratitude filled my heart as I said a silent prayer. *Thank You, Jesus. I couldn't have picked a better roommate in all the world.*

Mom and Betty remained kindred roommates until my mother's death in May of 1995. Betty told me that she was the last person to see Mom alive as Betty limped over to Mom's bedside to kiss her good morning.

Mom whispered, "Good-bye, Betty," and closed her eyes for the last time.

What a precious gift a good friend is, and what a Friend we have in Jesus.

After Mom's funeral, I came to get my painting of Jesus. Betty watched longingly as I removed it from the wall. "I just love that picture. It's such a comfort," she said, "especially since I miss Helen so much."

"Would you like to have the picture, Betty? I'm sure Mom would want you to have it."

Betty broke into a big smile. "Oh yes, I sure would!"

I hung the picture opposite her bed so she could easily see it. I told her how she had been an answer to my prayers. We hugged as I thanked her for being there for my mother. I promised to keep in touch as I took one last look at the picture of Jesus. Betty's bedside "roommate" was also the One who had answered my prayers.

Patricia prayed fervently for her mother during the last days of her life on this earth. The memories our moms leave behind are often carried in the fabric of the things they leave behind. So it was with Patricia's mom's quilt. Through it Patricia is forever reminded of the faithful prayers of her mother.

∿ My Mother's Floral Quilt ∿

BY PATRICIA WOLF, HARTFORD, WISCONSIN

My tired body felt some relief as I clutched the soft cotton fabric. I fingered the cross-stitched squares ever so gently, but the room's darkness made it impossible to make out the designs. It had been a long day of waiting, knowing Mom had little time left.

On the quilt there was a square for each of her grandchildren, and in the center of it a place for her, the grandma. I remembered the long hours I worked on designing and sewing the floral patterns on the Aida cloth. A flower, representing the month each grandchild was born, was sewn on each square, and his or her name had been added. A log-cabin patchwork was sewn around each piece to frame it. Then all the squares were sewn into strips, and the final quilt was born.

Her hug was warm the day she received the floral quilt that honored her grandchildren. She said it would enable her to keep them close to her heart. During bedtime she would pray for each child and for the daughter that had given her the cozy gift. Now I prayed that God would spare her pain and take her quickly, as her life was beginning to vanish.

Trying to fall into a sleep, I remembered my mom's antics in caring for the quilt that was now draped over my tired body. During the sunny times of the day, she would close the curtains so the sun would not damage the colors. During the hot months of summer, she would gently fold the quilt, package it, and tuck it into a closet. She hesitated to wash the quilt, until one day I volunteered to do the job and take all responsibility for fixing any damage done during its cleaning process. The quilt became a part of the fabric of her life and her prayers.

Too much sun spilled into Grandma's bedroom, and she insisted on keeping the quilt over the back of her couch in the living area. Daily her little grandchildren would visit her and eagerly look for treats. Sometimes they came for an easy time of talking about life. Other times they came to help clean or cook. Often one of the littlest would become tired and rest for a while on the couch. Grandma would softly spread the quilt over the child to keep the grandchild warm and whisper a prayer as she did.

Then Mom became sick and visits were now at the hospital. The quilt lay unused as busy days of traveling to and from the hospital replaced the family days at home. In a few short weeks, we knew she would soon be going home to be with Jesus, and now that day had come.

The decision was made to bring her back home to spend her last days of life. As the oxygen machines hummed, the grandchildren had all taken turns earlier that evening sitting at her bedside. They served as nurses, spending time wiping her brow or holding her hand. At one point, several grandsons surrounded her bed. On bended knee they prayed and waited. They waited like we all did, wondering if we could do more to help her and hoping for just a little more time to be with her.

Sleep overtook the grandchildren, and the room fell still of people's movements. The oxygen machines continued their profound hum. Still curled up on the couch, I hid beneath the layers of the quilt. Sweet memories flowed through my mind of times spent with Mom. The quilt was made to give her comfort, and now it brought me consolation during one of the darkest times of my life. "Oh, Lord, comfort me. This is too hard for me to handle on my own."

The morning light came. The colors of the quilt were alive and vivid to my tired eyes. People sounds filled the home, and the noise of the oxygen machines faded. Mom slept peacefully, and I decided to return home for the day. I had just entered the house when the phone rang. Tears streamed down my face as I listened to the caller. My prayers had been answered. Mama had quietly slipped away to go home to the Lord.

The funeral was beautiful. Each grandchild laid a red rose atop the coffin. A year later Grandpa died. The quilt has been carefully folded and tucked away in my closet. Though God's comfort has softened the pain of grief, memories are too fresh to have the quilt on display. Perhaps someday I will have my own grandchildren's quilt. At that time I may unfold the memories of Great-grandmother's quilt to the next generation. For a bundle of love has been sewn into the lives that my mother touched, while evening prayers were whispered to the Lord.

Not all moms are loving. Not all moms are kind. For those of us who, for one reason or another, have never been close to our own mom, prayer can be the means to close the gap of separation and heal the wounds.

∽ To Err Is Human; to Forgive, Divine ∾

BY TONYA RUIZ, GARDEN GROVE, CALIFORNIA

The ringing phone startled me awake. As I answered it, my dad said, "Your mom's in the emergency room. They think she's had a stroke."

Driving to the hospital, I felt sick to my stomach as I remembered our most recent phone conversation.

"Are you going to repaint your kitchen?" my mother had asked.

"I just painted it."

"But it looks pink."

"It's not pink, Mom. It's beige and it matches my tiles."

"Well, I couldn't live with a pink kitchen. Did Ron finish building the pantry?"

"No, he's been busy with work. He hasn't had time."

"I couldn't live without a pantry."

"I guess it's a good thing you don't live here, isn't it, Mom? I've gotta go."

Hanging up the phone, I had called my mother a name. My children stared at me with saucer eyes. I had never cussed in front of them before. Her critical spirit was so frustrating!

Walking into the hospital, I knew a good daughter would go straight to her mother's room, but I didn't. I detoured into the bathroom. Locking the stall door, I leaned against it and sobbed until I couldn't breathe. "Why does it have to be this way?" I asked God. "My mother is sick. I know I should go to her, but I can't. I just can't."

Then I prayed, "God, forgive me for my wrong attitude, and help me to forgive her for always being so critical and negative toward me. This may be the only chance I have to make peace with her, and I can't do this on my own. Please help me."

Leaning toward the little bathroom sink, I splashed cold water on my red, swollen face and braced myself for what was to come.

As I walked into the emergency room cubicle, I saw the woman who had given birth to me and I grieved, because I felt as if a wall separated us. I knew a loving daughter would rush in to hug and comfort her ailing mother.

Instead I said, "Hello, Mom," and turned my attention to the doctor. "Have you run any tests yet?"

"Psst…" My mother motioned for me to come over.

"What, Mom?"

Pointing to her lunch tray, she whispered, "Someone has stolen the cherries out of my fruit cocktail." She sounded like a little girl.

Obviously the stroke had affected her thinking.

While she acted childish, it was easy to be nice to her, but after a few days, as the swelling the stroke had caused in her brain subsided, her memory returned. One morning as I sat next to her bed, she was back to her old self.

"Isn't that the fattest nurse you've ever seen?"

"Ssshhh," I whispered.

"She can't hear me."

"She's overweight, Mom, not deaf."

"I don't know how she can do her job correctly."

"Gosh, Mom, did they diagnose you with a stroke or Tourette's syndrome?"

"Do I embarrass you?"

"Well," I said, collecting my stuff, "I had better get going."

As I was leaving her room, she called out, "I don't want any of those pastors from your church coming to visit me."

"Don't worry, Mom. They won't."

At home I told my husband, "It's a miracle she's still alive, and yet she is still so rebellious in her heart toward God. How can that be?"

My mother was a Christian from an early age and, on rare occasions, I had seen a fire for God burn in her heart. But it was quickly extinguished by the bitterness that permeated her life.

She was discharged from the hospital to recover at home, and I left town on a business trip. One ring of the hotel phone and I knew something was wrong before my dad said, "Tonya, you need to come home. Your mom's back in the hospital, and it doesn't look good."

Walking into the intensive care unit, I saw my mother dressed in a blue-checked gown and hooked up to monitors and IVs. She was receiving oxygen through a tube to ease her labored breathing. She reached out, held my hand, and said, "I'm afraid. Please don't leave me until I'm asleep."

One night as I sat next to her bed she said, "I'm so glad that this is happening to me and not to you."

Over the next few days, she introduced me to the nurses with, "Have you met my baby?"

When we were alone, she asked, "Tonya, what are they going to do now?"

"I don't know, Mom. There's a specialist who might be able to help you."

"What if he can't fix me?"

"Then you get to go to heaven first and wait for the rest of us. Is that okay?"

"You know, Tonya, you can get so sick that you don't care to live anymore."

"Do you have a peace about dying?"

She nodded her head and cried. I held on to the IV pole for support and wiped my tears with a crumpled Kleenex.

I brought her my CD player, and the sound of old "Beulah Land" and "I'd Rather Have Jesus" brought her comfort. She cried as she talked of relatives waiting for her in heaven: a father who had died when she was younger, and grandparents who were long since buried. She worried about leaving her 12 treasured grandchildren. Every time I left the room, she kissed me and said, "I love you." It had been a long time since I had heard those words.

The first time I ever heard my mother say "Praise the Lord" was in that hospital as she lay dying.

One morning when I arrived she asked, "Guess who came to visit me?"

"I don't have any idea, Mom. You had a visitor last night after I left?"

"Yes. Guess who?" she asked.

"I dunno. The president?"

"No. Your pastor!"

"Really?"

A cold sweat broke out. *Is she going to be mad at me?* I wondered. I began explaining. "Honestly, Mom, I didn't ask him to come."

"I know you didn't. He said he just decided to drop by."

"What happened? Did you throw your flowers at him?" I teased.

"It was really nice. We talked for a while and then we prayed."

"That's really good, Mom."

My mother was finally at peace with her Savior, but each day her physical condition went from bad to worse. Keeping a cool, wet cloth on her fevered forehead, I washed her and then put scented lotions on her thin frame. I held her hand as a single tear rolled down her cheek, and with her last breath I became motherless.

At her funeral a man shared what a sweet woman she had been. *He must not have known my mother,* I thought. I began remembering past wrongs and accusations, and I decided to wear my hurts like an old, tattered bathrobe. Months later I stood in the hall at home and stared at my family pictures hanging on the wall.

"Why am I smiling in all the pictures? I don't remember ever being happy as a child."

My husband took me into his arms and said, "Sweetheart, your mom is dead and buried. You need to get on with your life."

I called my lifelong friend. "Lisa, you knew my mother. Could I have done something different?"

"Tonya, you did everything you could."

"Maybe I didn't try hard enough to get along with her."

"Your mother was an extremely difficult person. You tried."

Mom's house was sold. As I was going through her things and packing them away, the scent of her filled the rooms and my mind with many forgotten memories. I found an old black-and-white picture of my beautiful young mother and myself as a toddler, cuddled together on the beach. As I sat staring at that faded photograph, I realized that my mother had not been perfect, but she did love me. I'm thankful that God answered my prayer from that emergency room bathroom stall. Because I was able to forgive my mother, we made peace before she died.

And I know she is waiting for me in heaven, even if she doesn't like the color of my kitchen.

Author Bios

Nancy C. Anderson (www.NancyCAnderson.com) is the author of *Avoiding the "Greener Grass" Syndrome: How to Grow Affair-Proof Hedges Around Your Marriage*. She is also a popular speaker at women's and couples' events. Nancy lives in California with her husband of 26 years and their son.

Peggie C. Bohanon, writer/editor and Web master of "Peggie's Place" (www.peggiesplace.com), has written for various publications and was a guest on Focus on the Family. Peggie's Place includes devotionals, a newsletter, and links to Christian/family resources. Peggie and her husband, Dr. Joseph Bohanon, reside in Springfield, Missouri.

Martha Bolton is an Emmy- and Dove-nominated writer and the author of over 50 books of humor, including *Didn't My Skin Used to Fit?* and *Cooking with Hot Flashes*. She was a staff writer for Bob Hope for 15 years, and is the popular Cafeteria Lady for *Brio* magazine.

Vicki Caruana, America's Teacher™, is the author of many books for parents and teachers. She writes to educate and encourage excellence in all of us. Visit her Web site at www.applesandchalkdust.com.

Jennifer Lynn Cary, an author, speaker, and teacher, is married to Phil and has three grown daughters (Jaime, Alyssa, and Meg), besides her giving son, Ian. Her novel *The Huguenot* uncovers the family lineage of her ancestor Davy Crockett.

Joan Clayton was named Woman of the Year 2003 in her city. She has written 7 books, been included in 47 anthologies, and has over 450 articles published in various publications. She is religion columnist for her local newspaper. Her Web site is www.joanclayton.com.

Sheila Corey, a published author, freelance writer, and speaker, and her husband, Marty Corey (a marriage and family therapist), are founders of the Merging Marriages Ministries. Together they conduct Merging Marriages and Families seminars. For workshop listings or topics visit www.mergingmarriage.com.

Ana Cormany, wife, mother, and friend writes about tough issues. She is passionate about equipping parents to face 21st-century realities, protecting children from sexual abuse, and encouraging survivors toward healing on this side of heaven. Email her at undeserveddisgrace@comcast.net.

Charlene Davis is an experienced freelance writer (www.cdavisfreelance.com), specializing in business, technical, and e-commerce. She is also a columnist for the *Pittsburgh Christian* newspaper. Her hobbies include scrapbooking, cooking, collecting recipes and vintage cookbooks, and maintaining her Web site for Christian women (www.busymomsrecipes.com).

Mary Ann L. Diorio, Ph.D. is an author, speaker, and life coach. She owns Life Coaching Consultants, LLC, in Millville, New Jersey, where she lives with her husband, Dominic. They are the blessed parents of two grown daughters, Lia and Gina. Mary Ann may be reached at www.LifeCoachingConsultants.us.

Susan Farr Fahncke is the author of *Angel's Legacy* and the co-author of and contributor to numerous other books. Susan also runs Angels2TheHeart, a foundation that sends care packages and cards to critically ill people. She lives in Utah and teaches on-line writing workshops. Visit her Web site at www.2TheHeart.com

Pam Farrel is an international speaker and author of over 20 books, including *Men Are Like Waffles, Women Are Like Spaghetti; The Treasure Inside Your Child;* and *10 Best Decisions a Woman Can Make.* She is Mom to three children and is happily married to Bill. Visit her Web sites at www.masterfulliving.com or www.farrelcommunications.com.

Carleta Fernandes lives in Amarillo, Texas, with husband, Rick. Retired after 20 years in law enforcement, she spends time reading about writing, talking about writing, and occasionally writing. Many of her stories are drawn from her life in police work and growing up a Texan.

Lana Fletcher lives in Chehalis, Washington, with her husband. They have one adult daughter. Their younger daughter was killed in a car accident. Lana is the church clerk, has attended Toastmasters for several years, and enjoys making Creative Memories albums, gardening, and writing.

Cheri Fuller is mother of three, an international speaker, and an award-winning author of over 30 books, including the bestselling *When Mothers Pray,* and *Fearless.* Honored as Oklahoma Mother of the Year 2004, Cheri has information about her ministry and a column for moms on her Web site at www.cherifuller.com.

Lynette Galisewski has a video-production company called Living Legacy Life History Chronicles in Littleton, Colorado. She loves to help people capture their values and beliefs in video or written form to pass along to loved ones. She is thankful to God for Braun's legacy!

Judy Gann is the author of *God of All Comfort: Devotions of Hope for Those Who Are Ill*, AMG Publishers/Living Ink Books, March 2005. Her passion is to comfort and encourage other people through her writing. An early-learning librarian, Judy lives in Lakewood, Washington.

Carol Genengels's stories have appeared in *Reminisce, Woman's Day, Stories for the Spirit Filled Believer, God Allows U-Turns,* and *Chicken Soup for the Soul.* Her book *Unfailing Love* details God's faithfulness amidst family tribulations. She and her husband live in the beautiful Pacific Northwest. Her Web site is awtcarolg@aol.com.

Nancy B. Gibbs is the author of four books, a contributor to numerous anthologies and national magazines, a weekly religion columnist for two newspapers, and a motivational speaker. Please visit her Web site at www.nancybgibbs.com or e-mail her at nancybgibbs@aol.com.

Carol Davis Gustke holds a bachelor of science degree in Human Services. Her slice-of-life stories have appeared in *Woman's World, Christian Singles,* and other top-selling magazines. Her first book, *Sacred Harvest*, was released in 2001. Visit her at www.carol gustke.com.

Anne C. Johnson is a wife, mother, freelance writer, and registered nurse. Her greatest joys in life are being a wife and mother; however, she has found that writing allows her to share her heart with more people. Through the stories she shares, Anne hopes to convey God's never-ending love.

Eileen Key, freelance author, resides in San Antonio, Texas, near her three children. Her writings are included in *Prayers and Promises for* *the Military, God's Way*, and other publications. She writes book reviews and is an editor for Moms in Print Publishers. Visit her Web site at www.key-writer.com.

Dr. Muriel Larson, author of 17 books and more than 7,500 first and reprinted published writings and songs, is a professional Christian writer, speaker, and e-mail counselor for two on-line publications, and has taught at writers conferences across the nation. For advice by e-mail, contact her at Doctormuriel@aol.com.

Lucinda Secrest McDowell, M.T.S., is a vibrant international conference speaker and author of five books, including *What We've Learned So Far, Amazed By Grace,* and *Quilts from Heaven.* A graduate of Gordon-Conwell Seminary, her ministry is "Encouraging Words that Transform!" Contact her at (860) 257-WORD or www.EncouragingWords.net.

Sandra McGarrity is the author of two Christian novels, *Woody* and *Caller's Spring.* Her writing has been published in volumes 3 and 4 of *God Allows U-Turns* and in many other publications. Visit her Web page at www.heartwarmers4u.com/members?woody.

Marcia Alice Mitchell lives in Salem, Oregon. She has sold over 250 articles and short stories to over 50 publications. Marcia is past president of the Oregon Christian Writers and has led a critique group in her home since 1990.

Paula Moldenhauer is a homeschooling mother of four. She loves hiking, hanging out with her children, and good conversation. Besides writing for magazines and book compilations, she has her own devotional e-zine. You can receive a free weekly e-devotion at her Web site, www.soulscents.us.

Toña Morales-Calkins is a writer and teacher. She lives in Northern California, where she is active in her faith community. *An Unlikely*

Expert is her second published story. She is currently at work on her sixth novel. She has no books published—yet.

Jessie Ann Moser lives in Wescosville, Pennsylvania, with her husband and daughter.

Marilyn Naseth and her husband, Drew, live in Faribault, Minnesota. They have three grown children. Marilyn is an independent consultant for Good Books and Company. She enjoys reading and writing and is a published author. She also enjoys volunteer and service opportunities.

Ginger K. Nelson graduated from College Misericordia in Dallas, Pennsylvania, and is devoted to her husband, Fritz, and her children: Linda, Fen, Danny, and Misty. She has published two books: *Pirates Revenge*, a children's ghost story, and a biography of her special-needs son, *They'll Remember Our Son*.

Jeanne Pallos is the author of several published stories and enjoys leading a writers' critique group in Orange County, California. A former schoolteacher, she lives in Laguna Niguel with her husband and two dogs. Jeanne can be reached at jlpallos@cox.net.

Vickie Pape—Author requests no biography.

Susan Peabody is a writer and teacher who likes helping people feel better about themselves and about life. Her books include *Addiction to Love: Overcoming Obsession and Dependency in Relationships* and *The Art of Changing*. Her Web site is www.brightertomorrow.net.

Dr. Debra Peppers, Emmy-award-winning author, television/radio host, and speaker, has traveled to 50 states and 50 foreign countries. Featured in *Chicken Soup, God Allows U-Turns*, and her own book, *It's Your Turn, Now*, Debra is available for speaking and can be contacted at 314-842-7425 or www.saltandlightministry.com.

Gloria Helen Plaistad and husband, Rick, enjoy being lovebirds in an empty nest in Two Harbors, Minnesota, where they are celebrating 33 years of marriage. They have three children and ten grandchildren. Along with being coentrepreneurs in their business, Gloria is also a busy author and speaker.

Shirley Rose is the author of four books and has contributed stories for numerous others. She is the executive producer and cohost of the Emmy-nominated women's television program *Aspiring Women*, which is seen across the United States and in several foreign countries. Shirley has three children and six grandchildren.

Tonya Ruiz is a dynamic communicator, actress, and Bible teacher who speaks nationally about some of today's most important issues. She is a pastor's wife, mother, and grandmother who calls Southern California home. Her Web site is www.BeautyQuest.net.

Kim Vogel Sawyer is a wife, mother, grandmother, teacher, writer, and speaker who loves *C* words like *cats, children, chocolate, choir, church,* and *Connor* (her grandson's name). At home in Kansas, Kim enjoys quilting and calligraphy, and she is an avid reader and writer. Her Web site is www.KimVogelSawyer.com.

Patricia Sheets is a freelance writer with an offbeat sense of humor. She lives in Virginia Beach, Virginia, with the three men in her life. Jack, her husband, is a pastor. Duncan and Barkley are pound-saved mutts, but nonetheless her "boys."

Debbie Hannah Skinner is a "Bible teacher with a paintbrush" living in Amarillo, Texas, with her husband and daughter. Founder of Mirror Ministries, she weaves her words with watercolors and wisdom from Scripture in a nationwide teaching ministry to women. Contact her at www.dhskinner.com.

Cori Smelker is a mother to five kids and wife to one husband. She is passionate about the Lord and wants her writing to glorify Him in all avenues. She is generally found at her desk, surrounded by dogs, a cat, and a ball python.

Dee Smith retired in 1995 and was an actress for TV and stage, taught acting to children, and is now working as a full-time writer. She lives in Houston, Texas, and has three children: Michael, Gary, and Vicki, and a grandson, Hayden.

Karen Strand's articles have appeared in *Moody Magazine, Focus on the Family,* and *Today's Christian Woman,* among other publications. She is the author of *Escape From the Fowler's Snare,* which is profiled on her Web site at www.karenstrand.com.

Kathleen Szitas lives in Greensboro, North Carolina, with her sons, Steven and Sean, and husband, Rob. She is a substitute English teacher and an aspiring writer of children's books and Christian dramas. She loves to read and is active in the children's ministry at her church.

Amy Wallace is blessed to be a wife and the mother of three amazing children. She writes Christian fiction specifically for moms based on vivid experiences from 11 years of classroom and homeschool teaching combined. She is a member of American Christian Romance Writers.

Anne Culbreath Watkins is the author of *The Conure Handbook* (Barron's Educational Series, Inc.). Her writing has appeared in numerous publications. She and her husband, Allen, live in Alabama where they enjoy spoiling their grandchildren: Bailey, Chelsea, and Tyler. Her Web site is www.geocities.com/anne_c_watkins.

Sharen Watson: see "About Our Editors" on page 214.

PeggySue Wells, writer and speaker, has authored several titles including the What to Do series, featuring *What to Do When You Don't Want to Go to Church* and *What to Do When You Don't Know What to Say*. Her articles appear nationally.

Kari West, author of *When He Leaves: Help and Hope for Hurting Women*, is an inspirational speaker and founder of Take Hope to Heart™ Ministries. Subscribe to her *DivorceWise Newsletter* at www.GardenGlories.com or by writing her at P. O. Box 11692, Pleasanton, CA 94568. For booking information, contact www.TakeHopeToHeart.com.

Patricia Wolf is publisher for *CHATTELS of the Heart,* an inspirational publication since 2001, one of the moderators for Christian Writers Fellowship International's FORUM, and a sponsor of the Wisconsin PAW Writer's Conference. Information regarding future writers conferences can be found at www.4safeinternet.net/~chattelstheheart/

About Our Editors

Allison Bottke is the founder of the God Allows U-Turns Project, and lead editor in all the books developed under this popular umbrella brand. Allison frequently speaks at women's events and writing conferences around the country. Visit her web site for more information on Allison and the exciting U-Turns outreach. www.godallowsuturns.com

Cheryll M. Hutchings is co-editor and administrative assistant of the popular God Allows U-Turns Project, an international outreach ministry founded by Allison Bottke. A Christian since the age of 12, Cheryll has always let God lead her in life. The best adventure He's led her on so far has been joining the God Allows U-Turns Project on the ground floor of the ministry when it began in 2000. Reading countless stories submitted by contributing authors from around the world, Cheryll was instrumental in the development and editing of the first four books in the God Allows U-Turns series, as well as the most recent books in the new God Answers Prayers series. Married to Bob for 27 years, they have a 22-year-old son Aaron, who is working full time in the computer industry, and a 19-year-old son Scott, who is a Corporal in the Marine Corps. They live in the country in a rambling ranch in Medina, Ohio, sitting in several acres of peaceful seclusion, surrounded by the Lord's beautiful nature and wildlife.

Sharen Watson resides in Spring, TX (with Denver, CO fast approaching) with Ray, her college sweetheart and "most supportive" husband of 24 years. They have a married daughter, one son in college, another son in high school, and one spoiled Lhasa Apso. Sharen is Founder/Director of Words for the Journey Christian Writer's Guild. She also leads women's Bible studies and speaks her testimony of God's enduring faithfulness and love. Her desire is that every word she speaks and writes will be a reflection of God's hope, restoration, and joy. You can visit her web site at *www.Wordsforthe Journey.org*

Ten Tips on How to Pray

1. Set aside a short time each day to meet with God. Yes, God hears our short "bullet prayers" throughout the day, but true fellowship wants more than that. Keep your appointment with God, just as you would any other appointment. Start by making these divine encounters brief. Even five minutes a day is a great start. You can add more time once the habit is established.

2. If you feel awkward at first, or your mind wanders, or you get a bit sleepy, do not feel guilty. God understands. Take a moment to read a few verses from the Psalms or the day's entry in your favorite daily devotional book. It may take time to get used to being in the presence of God.

3. Ask God to help you pray. Prayer is, after all, His invention. He designed prayer as the means for us to communicate with Him. Let Him be your Teacher.

4. One very good place to start praying is to simply confess any known sin to God and claim His forgiveness. At this same time, be sure you harbor no bitterness toward anyone else. Unforgiveness can hinder your prayers. If a specific person with whom you have hard feelings comes to mind, ask God to forgive

you and change your heart. If necessary, go to the other person and make things right.

5. Remember, prayer is more than asking for things. God loves it when we just take time to praise Him for who He is and thank Him for the blessings He has given us.

6. If you are likely to forget what you want to pray about, start a small, written prayer list where you jot down the things for which you want to pray.

7. Some people find it useful to actually write out their prayers and keep a journal of when and how God answers. For others, a journal may seem a distraction. Try it and see if it works for you.

8. Look for other opportunities to pray throughout the day. Waiting in line at the supermarket, washing the dishes, sitting in traffic…these are all excellent times to talk to God.

9. Remember the stories when people asked God to use them to touch another life? Ask God to do the same through you. Then watch for the divine appointments He will set up throughout the day.

10. Above all, consider your time with God a call to *joy*, not some staid, dry, religious exercise. Learn to delight in God as you pray. He delights in you!

About the God Allows
U-Turns Project ®

ALONG WITH THESE EXCITING new Answered Prayer books published by Harvest House, we want to share with readers the entire scope of the powerful God Allows U-Turns outreach of hope and healing.

The broad outreach of this organization includes the book you now hold in your hands, as well as other nonfiction and fiction books for adults, youth, and children. Written by Allison Gappa Bottke, along with other collaborating authors and coeditors, there are currently 14 books available under the God Allows U-Turns umbrella brand, with 5 additional books releasing in 2005 and 2006, including Allison's first novel in the "chick-lit" genre.

More than 50,000 copies of the God Allows U-Turns tract, featuring Allison's powerful testimony of making a U-turn toward God, have been distributed around the world.

There is a line of nine God Allows U-Turns greeting cards touching on difficult times when new direction is needed. Also available is an entire line of merchandise featuring the highly recognizable God Allows U-Turns signature yellow road sign, items such as Bible book covers, ball caps, and such. Also in development is a God Allows U-Turns TV interview talk show and a national speakers tour.

Sharing the life-saving message that you can never be so lost or so broken that you cannot turn toward God is Allison's main passion in her life and in her ministry.

Visit your local bookstore or the God Allows U-Turns Web site (www.godallowsuturns.com) to find out more about this exciting ministry that is helping to change lives or write:

Allison Bottke
The God Allows U-Turns Project
P.O. Box 717
Faribault, MN 55021-0717
editor@godallowsuturns.com

The God Allows U-Turns Foundation®

One of the most profound lessons in the Bible is that of giving. The Holy Bible is quite clear in teaching us how we are to live our lives. Scripture refers to this often, and never has the need to share with other people been so great.

Give, and it will be given to you. A good measure, pressed down, shaken together and running over, will be poured into your lap. For with the measure you use, it will be measured to you (Luke 6:38).

In keeping with the lessons taught us by the Lord our God, we are pleased to have the opportunity to donate a portion of the net profits of every God Allows U-Turns book to one or more nonprofit Christian charity. These donations are made through the God Allows U-Turns Foundation, a funding mechanism established by Kevin and Allison Bottke as a way to share the success of the growing U-Turns outreach ministry.

For more details visit the Web site at
www.godallowsuturns.com.

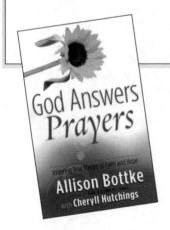